Presented to

Marie

From

Sue

Date

5/1/16
Happy 60th !

EVERYDAY

Prayers
& Praises

A Daily Devotional
for Women

Rachel Quillin and Vicki J. Kuyper

BARBOUR
PUBLISHING

Scripture quotations, unless otherwise noted, are taken from the King James Version of the Bible.

Scripture quotations marked NIV are taken from the HOLY BIBLE, NEW INTERNATIONAL VERSION®. NIV®. Copyright © 1973, 1978, 1984, 2011 by Biblica, Inc.™ Used by permission. All rights reserved worldwide.

Scripture quotations marked CEV are from the Contemporary English Version, Copyright © 1995 by American Bible Society. Used by permission.

Scripture quotations marked NKJV are taken from the New King James Version®. Copyright © 1982 by Thomas Nelson, Inc. Used by permission. All rights reserved.

Scripture quotations marked MSG are from **THE MESSAGE.** Copyright © by Eugene H. Peterson 1993, 1994, 1995, 1996, 2000, 2001, 2002. Used by permission of NavPress Publishing Group.

Scripture quotations marked NLT are taken from the *Holy Bible,* New Living Translation, copyright © 1996, 2004, 2007 by Tyndale House Foundation. Used by permission of Tyndale House Publishers, Inc. Carol Stream, Illinois 60188. All rights reserved.

Scripture quotations marked NCV are taken from the New Century Version of the Bible, copyright © 2005 by Thomas Nelson, Inc. Used by permission.

Scripture quotations marked ESV are from The Holy Bible, English Standard Version®, copyright © 2001 by Crossway Bibles, a publishing ministry of Good News Publishers. Used by permission. All rights reserved.

Scripture quotations marked NASB are taken from the New American Standard Bible, © 1960, 1962, 1963, 1968, 1971, 1972, 1973, 1975, 1977, 1995 by The Lockman Foundation. Used by permission.

Scripture marked GNT taken from the Good News Translation® (Today's English Standard Version, Second Edition) Copyright © 1992 by American Bible Society. Used by Permission.

Published by Barbour Books, an imprint of Barbour Publishing, Inc., P.O. Box 719, Uhrichsville, Ohio 44683, www.barbourbooks.com

Our mission is to publish and distribute inspirational products offering exceptional value and biblical encouragement to the masses.

Member of the
Evangelical Christian
Publishers Association

Printed in China.

Introduction

EVERYDAY PRAYERS AND PRAISES

*Draw nigh to God,
and he will draw nigh to you.*

JAMES 4:8

This lovely daily devotional offers just-right-sized readings that are a perfect fit for your busy lifestyle. These 365 devotional readings feature themes that are important to your heart—including faith, friendship, generosity, grace, love, rest, happiness, peace, self-esteem, and dozens more. As you move through the pages of *Everyday Prayers and Praises*, you'll be encouraged and inspired every day of the year as you experience the refreshing peace and assurance that can only be found through an intimate relationship with the Master Creator.

Godly Examples

*Let your heart therefore be perfect
with the LORD our God, to walk
in his statutes, and to keep his
commandments, as at this day.*

1 KINGS 8:61

I've seen quite a few examples of godly people, and I'm so thankful You've allowed them to cross my path, Father. It's a real encouragement to see other people who are becoming more and more like You. It helps me in my own quest for Christlikeness. Thank You for bringing these individuals into my life.

Gift of Grace

GOD is good to one and all;
everything he does is
suffused with grace.

PSALM 145:9 MSG

If a driver in front of you unexpectedly pays your toll, you can't help but feel in her debt. It's a kindness you didn't deserve and can't repay. Jesus' death on the cross was more than a random act of kindness. It was part of an eternal plan. It was also a gift of grace. Jesus paid a high toll for your sins. You can't repay Him. All you can do is gratefully accept what He's given.

My Church Family

For we are members of his body,
of his flesh, and of his bones.

EPHESIANS 5:30

My church is special to me in so many ways, Lord. I am so thankful that You have placed me among such a wonderful group of believers who encourage me and pray for me. Allow me to be a blessing to them as well, and help me to never forget how important they are in my life.

For Each New Day

*But seek ye first the kingdom of God,
and his righteousness; and all these
things shall be added unto you.*

MATTHEW 6:33

Every day there is something for which
I can offer You praise, dear God! To begin
with, we have the promise of a fresh start—
a new opportunity to serve You. Throughout
the day You show Your majesty in a multi-
tude of ways. You are an awesome God!

Precious People

Since thou wast precious in my sight,
thou hast been honourable, and I have
loved thee: therefore will I give men for
thee, and people for thy life.

ISAIAH 43:4

There are many precious people who offer their time and talents for You, Lord Jesus. I just want to thank You for each one. I appreciate those who make a public contribution as well as those who work behind the scenes. They mean more to me than I can say.

DAY 6

All He Has

*All sunshine and sovereign is GOD,
generous in gifts and glory.*
PSALM 84:11 MSG

You have a Father who owns the cattle on a thousand hills and holds the cosmos in His hands. This Almighty Father generously offers all He has to you. He offers you a life overflowing with joy, comfort, and blessing. But like any gift, this one has to be accepted before it can be enjoyed. Today, why not say yes to the Father who loves you? Tell Him how you long to live—and love—like His cherished child.

God's Goodness

I would have lost heart, unless I had believed that I would see the goodness of the Lord in the land of the living.

PSALM 27:13 NKJV

Knowing a friend's heart toward you can help you relax and be yourself. With a friend like this, you can honestly share your deepest secrets, feelings, and failures without fear of ridicule or reprisal. The psalms remind us over and over again that God's heart toward us is good. Believing in God's innate goodness means we can entrust every detail of our lives to Him without hesitation.

The Center of God's Will

And he said, The God of our fathers hath chosen thee, that thou shouldest know his will, and see that Just One, and shouldest hear the voice of his mouth.

Acts 22:14

Lord, I know that in the center of Your will are peace, joy, and many other rich blessings. I'd like to experience all these things, but the trouble I seem to have is figuring out what Your will is for me. Please help me be attentive when You speak, and give me a heart willing to be used by You.

Fashioned with Love

*I praise you because I am
fearfully and wonderfully made.*

PSALM 139:14 NIV

You are a living, breathing reason for praise. God formed only one of you, unique in appearance, intricate in design, priceless beyond measure. You were fashioned with both love and forethought. When you look in the mirror, is this what you reflect upon? If not, it's time to retrain your brain. Use the mirror as a touchstone to praise. Ask God, "What do You see when You look at me?" Listen quietly as God's truth helps retool your self-image.

Attitude Adjustment

This is the day the Lord has made;
we will rejoice and be glad in it.

PSALM 118:24 NKJV

What kind of day will you have today? Your answer might be, "I won't know until I've lived it!" But the attitude with which you approach each new day can change the way you experience life. That's why it's important to set aside some "attitude adjustment time" every morning. When you wake, remind yourself, "This is the day the Lord has made." Look for His hand in the details, and thank Him for every blessing He brings your way.

Day 11

What Do You Believe?

*You have always been God—long before
the birth of the mountains, even before
you created the earth and the world.*

PSALM 90:2 CEV

People once believed the world was flat. This meant only the most intrepid explorers would venture long distances and risk falling off the "edge" of the earth. What people believe determines the choices they make, no matter what era they live in. What do you believe about God? Does it line up with what the Bible says? It's worth checking out. Since you will live what you believe, it's important to be certain what you believe is true.

17

Your Favorite Meal

*You thrill to GOD's Word, you
chew on Scripture day and night.*

PSALM 1:2 MSG

Imagine God's words as your favorite meal, each bite a delicacy to be savored and enjoyed. You relish the unique blend of ingredients, the flavor and texture. When the meal is complete, you're nourished and satisfied. Scripture is a well-balanced meal for your heart and soul, a meal that can continue long after your Bible is back on the shelf. Ponder what you've read. Meditate on God's promises. Chew on the timeless truths that add zest to your life.

A Shower Every Day

I said to myself, "Relax and rest.
GOD has showered you with blessings."

PSALM 116:7 MSG

Friends know what friends need," so the
saying goes. That's one reason why friends
often throw celebratory showers for brides
and moms-to-be. It's a way to help provide
what a new wife or mom will need in the
months to come. God knows us, and our
needs, better than any friend or family member. That's why He throws us a shower every
day. God wraps His blessings in wisdom,
purpose, and creativity to help meet our
physical, emotional, and spiritual needs.

Always Has Been, Always Will Be

The LORD will watch over your coming and going both now and forevermore.

PSALM 121:8 NIV

Conventional wisdom tells us that nothing lasts forever. Thankfully, just because a saying is often quoted doesn't make it true. The time-tested wisdom of the Bible assures us that God always has been and always will be. Because of Jesus, forever is a word that can apply to us as well. When we follow Jesus here on earth, we follow Him straight to heaven. We have the assurance of knowing our true life span is "forevermore."

Difficult Things

Our Lord is great, with limitless strength; we'll never comprehend what he knows and does. God puts the fallen on their feet again.

PSALM 147:5–6 MSG

During a track and field event, it isn't uncommon to see an athlete trip over one of the hurdles and tumble to the ground. What brings the crowd to its feet is when the runner gets back up. Challenge involves risk, in sports and in life. Don't be afraid of trying difficult things. Whether you succeed or fail, God promises to renew your strength and purpose. You may not understand how, but you can be certain He's able.

Today, Tomorrow, Always

*But what the LORD has
planned will stand forever.
His thoughts never change.*

PSALM 33:11 CEV

Our God isn't wishy-washy. He doesn't experience bad hair days or mood swings, nor is He swayed by trends, fads, or peer pressure. Our perfect, eternal God has no peer. From scripture we can tell that God experiences emotions like love, grief, and pleasure. However, He isn't driven by His emotions, as we sometimes are. That means we can trust God to be true to His promises, His plans, and His character—today, tomorrow, and always.

Heaven-Sent

Children are a heritage from the LORD,
offspring a reward from him.

PSALM 127:3 NIV

A child is a gift that is literally heaven-sent. You don't have to have children of your own to care about the kids around you—or to learn from them. In the New Testament, Jesus talks about how our faith should resemble that of a child's. To understand why, consider this: Children believe what they hear, love unconditionally, and say what they think. What a wonderful way to relate to God.

Bridegroom and Friend

GOD's a safe-house for the battered,
a sanctuary during bad times.
The moment you arrive, you relax;
you're never sorry you knocked.

PSALM 9:9–10 MSG

When women are in need of comfort, they seem to instinctively turn to a spouse or close friend. There's nothing wrong with seeking a human shoulder to cry on when you need it. Just remember that the Bible refers to Jesus as both our bridegroom and friend. The comfort God provides runs deeper than anything people can offer. God sees your problems as part of a larger, eternal picture and can offer perspective as well as solace.

Think on Pure Things

*Blessed are the pure in heart:
for they shall see God.*

MATTHEW 5:8

Dear heavenly Father, there's just not much in today's society that encourages purity, but Your Word certainly demonstrates the importance of focusing our attention upon things that are pure. From experience, I have learned that life is more satisfying when it's geared toward pleasing You rather than the flesh, and I thank You for these lessons.

Love in Action

*As a father has compassion on
his children, so the LORD has
compassion on those who fear him.*

PSALM 103:13 NIV

If your children are hurting, you don't think twice about coming to their aid. You listen attentively to their heartaches, dry their tears, and offer them words of wisdom and encouragement. As God's child, you have a perfect and powerful heavenly Father who feels this way about you. His compassion is more than emotion. It's love in action. You can tell God anything, without fear of condemnation or abandonment. God's forgiveness runs as deep as His love.

Never Doubt

My heart is confident in you,
O God; my heart is confident.
No wonder I can sing your praises!

PSALM 57:7 NLT

In the Bible, when a word or phrase is repeated, it's time to pay attention. In the original language of the Old Testament, this signifies that something is the best, the ultimate, the pièce de résistance! The psalmist in Psalm 57 doubly notes how confident his heart is in God. No wonder praise comes naturally to him! Take it from the psalmist: You need never doubt God's heart toward you. You can be confident—eternally confident—in Him.

Follow His Lead

The LORD is my shepherd, I lack nothing.
PSALM 23:1 NIV

When it comes to brains, sheep are not the sharpest crayons in the box. They frighten easily, tend to follow the crowd, and have limited abilities for defending themselves. That's why sheep thrive best with a shepherd who guides, protects, and cares for their needs. Our Good Shepherd will do the same for us. Worry, fear, and discontent are products of a sheepish mentality. However, the peace of true contentment can be ours when we follow God's lead.

Bold and Courageous

When I called, you answered me;
you greatly emboldened me.

PSALM 138:3 NIV

Women are often characterized as timid creatures—fleeing from spiders, screaming over mice, cowering behind big, burly men when danger is near. But the Bible characterizes women of God as bold and courageous. Queen Esther risked her life to save God's children from genocide. Deborah led an army and judged the tribes of Israel. Rahab dared to hide Jewish spies to save her family. Today God will supply the courage you need to accomplish whatever He's asked you to do.

Unique Paths

And God is able to make all grace
abound toward you; that ye, always
having all sufficiency in all things,
may abound to every good work.

2 CORINTHIANS 9:8

Your desire is that we seek and do Your will, dear God, but You'll never force us to do it. You've laid unique paths before each of us, and it's because You love us all in a special way. Help us not to envy Your plans for others; let us complete our work with joy.

Labor of Love

*I will walk in freedom, for I have
devoted myself to your commandments.*

PSALM 119:45 NLT

Being devoted to someone you love is one
thing. Being devoted to doing something,
like completing a project or following God's
commandments, is quite another. It doesn't
sound as passionate or pleasurable, but
devoting yourself to do what God asks isn't
a self-improvement program. It's a labor
of love. Commitment is a way of expressing
love, whether it's honoring your marriage
vows or devoting yourself to doing what's
right. Love is a verb, always in action, making invisible emotions visible.

Solid Ground

*Those who trust in the LORD are like
Mount Zion, which cannot be
shaken but endures forever.*

PSALM 125:1 NIV

Alpine peaks endure sun and showers,
heat and hail. They don't yield or bow to
adverse conditions, but continue to stand
firm, being exactly what God created them
to be—majestic mountains. God created you
to be a strong, victorious woman. You were
designed to endure the changing seasons of
this life with God's help. Lean on Him when
the winds of life begin to blow. God and His
Word are solid ground that will never shift
beneath your feet.

Great Things!

Be brave. Be strong. Don't give up.
Expect GOD to get here soon.
PSALM 31:24 MSG

Trusting God can help transform you into
a "glass half-full" kind of person. You can
face every day, even the tough ones, with
confidence and expectation because you're
aware there's more to this life than can be
seen. You can rest in the promise that God
is working all things together for your good.
You know death is not the end. In other
words, you can expect that great things lay
ahead. Why not anticipate them with thanks
and praise?

Worthy of Service

*Not by works of righteousness
which we have done, but according
to his mercy he saved us, by the
washing of regeneration, and
renewing of the Holy Ghost.*

TITUS 3:5

You wanted to use me, Father, but You knew there were areas in my heart that first needed cleansing. You knew the only way to accomplish this would be to send purifying flames. The testing fires were painful some-times, but I'm glad You sent them. It felt good to be washed and worthy of service.

The One Who Knows You

Look at him; give him your warmest smile. Never hide your feelings from him.

PSALM 34:5 MSG

People often ask, "How are you?" as a formality. What they want to hear is "Fine!" Nothing more. But God wants more than a passing acquaintance with you. He invites you to share not only what you want and need, but also how you feel. God created you as a woman with complex emotions. You need never hesitate to share your tears, or even a hormonal outburst, with the One who knows you and loves you through and through.

Perfectly Forgiving

*You, Lord, are forgiving and good,
abounding in love to all who call to you.*

PSALM 86:5 NIV

The fact that God is perfect can be intimidating, especially when you consider that God knows everything you've ever done. But our perfect God is also perfectly forgiving. There is nothing you can do, or have done, that will make Him turn away from you. When you ask for forgiveness, you have it. No groveling. No begging. All you need to do is come to Him in humility and truth. Jesus has taken care of the rest.

Loving Friends

*And these God-chosen lives
all around—what splendid
friends they make!*

PSALM 16:3 MSG

Thank God for friendship. Literally. Spending time with those who understand how you tick, remind you what a wonderful woman you are, and challenge you to reach your God-given potential is one of life's greatest joys. The best way to have great friends is to be one. Pray regularly for the women God brings into your life, asking God to help you love them in ways that help you grow closer to each other and to Him.

Your Story

*All the days ordained for me were
written in your book before
one of them came to be.*

PSALM 139:16 NIV

The story of your life is written one day at
a time. Every choice you make influences
the chapters yet to come. But one thing is
certain—the ending. Your future was written
the moment you chose to follow God. That
means the end of your story here on earth is
actually a brand-new beginning. It's a story
with endless chapters, a "happy eternally
after" where tears are history and true love
never fails.

A Broken Heart

These things I have spoken unto you,
that in me ye might have peace.
In the world ye shall have tribulation:
but be of good cheer; I have
overcome the world.

JOHN 16:33

I know You understand grief better than anyone else, Father, but right now I feel as if no one has traveled this road before. My sorrow is so deep, my pain so intense. It seems I'm all alone. I need You, God. My soul cries out for relief. Please heal my broken heart, and help me smile once more.

A Glimpse of God's Goodness

Worship God if you want the best;
worship opens doors to all his goodness.

PSALM 34:9 MSG

In the Old Testament book of Exodus we read about Moses, a man God referred to as "friend." When Moses asks to see God's glory, God shows Moses His goodness. Afterward, Moses' face literally glows. When we worship God, we glimpse His goodness. We focus on who He is, what He's done, and what He's promised is yet to come. Our faces may not glow like Moses', but glimpsing God's goodness is bound to bathe our hearts in joy.

Wrapped in Grace

For the LORD God is our sun and our
shield. He gives us grace and glory.
The LORD will withhold no good thing
from those who do what is right.

PSALM 84:11 NLT

When a gift is wrapped in grace, it comes
with no strings attached. That's the kind of
gift God gives. He doesn't hold eternal life
just out of reach, taunting, "If you try
harder, this can be yours." He doesn't promise to love us if we never mess up again. He
doesn't say He'll forgive, but refuse to forget.
God graces us with gifts we don't deserve,
because His love is deeper than our hearts
and minds can comprehend.

Day 36

Wonder and Adventure

The LORD says, "I will guide you along the best pathway for your life. I will advise you and watch over you."

PSALM 32:8 NLT

If you're on safari, a knowledgeable guide will lead you to the best vantage point to see wildlife, educate you on what you're seeing, and protect you from danger. God is like a safari guide who never leaves your side. He knows both the joys and the dangers that surround you. Through His Spirit and scripture, God will guide you toward a life of wonder and adventure. Stay close to His side and allow Him to lead.

A Happy Heart

Live a happy life! Keep your eyes
open for GOD, watch for his works;
be alert for signs of his presence.

PSALM 105:3–4 MSG

Babies often smile when they catch sight of
their mother's face. Catching a glimpse of
God can do the same for us. It can make our
hearts happy. Yet God's presence is much
more subtle than that of a human parent.
God reveals Himself in quiet ways, such as
in an answer to prayer, the glory of a sunset,
or the gift of a new friend. Keep your eyes
open. God is ever present and at work in
your life.

The Impossible

Do something, LORD God, and use your powerful arm to help those in need.

PSALM 10:12 CEV

God spoke the cosmos into being. He fashioned the ebb and flow of the tides. He breathed life into what was once nothing more than dust. This same awesome God is reaching down to offer His help to you today. Perhaps your prayer is for your own needs. Or maybe it's for those you care about but don't know how to help. God is mighty enough, and loving enough, to do the impossible.

No Better Friend

*Jesus answered and said unto him,
If a man love me, he will keep my
words: and my Father will love him,
and we will come unto him,
and make our abode with him.*

JOHN 14:23

Dear Jesus, I've known many people in my life. I've enjoyed many good relationships and tried to avoid the bad. One thing is certain though. My relationship with You is the most important. I'm so glad You have time for me and that You want me to fellowship with You. I couldn't ask for a better friend.

God's Best

*Happy is he who has the God
of Jacob for his help, Whose hope
is in the LORD his God.*

PSALM 146:5 NKJV

Some people place their hope in financial security. Others hope their popularity, abilities, or connections will get them where they want to go. Still others hope that if they want something badly enough, it'll just happen. But only those who place their hope in God can face tomorrow without any fear of the future. When you trust in God, you do more than hope for the best. You rest in knowing God's best is His plan for your life.

A Welcome Reminder

Where morning dawns, where evening fades, you call forth songs of joy.

PSALM 65:8 NIV

Happiness is usually the result of circumstance. Joy, however, bubbles up unbidden, often persisting in spite of circumstance. It's an excitement that simmers below the surface, an assurance that God is working behind the scenes, a contentment that deepens as you discover your place in the world. The more at home you feel with God, the more joy will make a home in your heart—a welcome reminder that God is near.

DAY 42

Leaders in Life

*You guided your people like a flock
of sheep, and you chose Moses
and Aaron to be their leaders.*

PSALM 77:20 CEV

Think of the leaders in your life. The list
may include a boss, pastor, Bible study
leader, mentor, chairperson, or the govern-
ment officials helping steer the direction of
the country you live in. The Bible encourages
us to support and pray for our leaders. It
doesn't add a disclaimer, saying this applies
only if we like them, agree with them, or
voted for them. How would God have you
pray for your leaders today?

The Power of Words

*Words of wisdom come when good
people speak for justice.*

PSALM 37:30 CEV

It takes courage to stand up for what's
right, especially if you're the only voice
speaking up in the crowd. But words have
power. They can help bring injustice to
light. They can encourage others to take
a stand. They can incite change. But the
right motive is just as important as the right
words. Ephesians 4:15 tells us to speak "the
truth in love." Truth tempered with love is
the perfect agent of change.

DAY 44

In Charge of Relationships

*He that loveth his brother abideth
in the light, and there is none
occasion of stumbling in him.*

1 JOHN 2:10

Lord, I generally think of relationships as
being between people, and I fail to
remember that my relationship to things
can seriously affect how I react to people.
For instance, sometimes I get so involved in
a television show that I fail to give needed
attention to my family. Forgive me, Father.
Be in charge of my relationships.

More Than Results

*Discover for yourself that the
Lord is kind. Come to him for
protection, and you will be glad.*

PSALM 34:8 CEV

Kindness turns criticism into encouragement, bad news into words of comfort,
and discipline into teachable moments.
That's because kindness is concerned with
more than results. It's also concerned with
people's hearts. God's plan for you is bigger
than being a "good person." God also wants
you to be healed and whole. You can trust
God to be a loving Father and not a callous
taskmaster, because the breadth of His
kindness stems from the depth of His love.

New Beginnings

You turned my wailing into dancing;
you removed my sackcloth and
clothed me with joy.

PSALM 30:11 NIV

Some seasons of life pull you into the shadows. But God wants to help you make your way back into the light—not because you shouldn't mourn, but because every season heralds a new beginning. There is joy ahead, even if you can't see it or feel it right now. Each day brings you closer to those first flutters of joy. Watch for them. Wait for them. Pray for them. Then celebrate their arrival with thanks and praise.

Keeping Focus

The LORD is there to rescue all who are
discouraged and have given up hope.

PSALM 34:18 CEV

It's easy to lose heart when your focus is on difficulties that persist day after day. That's why reconnecting with God every morning is so important. Time together reminds you that an all-knowing and all-powerful God is in your corner, ready and able to help. It helps you sift the trivial from the eternal. And it restores hope to its rightful place in your life, where it can shine a light on God's goodness and faithfulness to you.

53

Time to Rest

*Take my yoke upon you, and learn of me;
for I am meek and lowly in heart: and ye
shall find rest unto your souls.*

MATTHEW 11:29

I find it difficult to even sit down to a meal,
Father. Resting seems like such a far-fetched
notion. I know You want me to find time to
rest and spend time with You, but I'm on the
go constantly, and I still don't get everything
done. Please help me, Lord, to make resting
a priority.

Hope and Healing

*My health may fail, and my spirit may
grow weak, but God remains the strength
of my heart; he is mine forever.*

PSALM 73:26 NLT

Your body is amazingly resilient, yet
terminally fragile. Fashioned by God's lov-
ingly creative hand, it was not designed to
last. But you were. That's because you are so
much more than your body. But God cares
about all of you, your body and your soul.
Even if your health fails, He will not. He is
near. He hears every prayer, even those you
hesitate to pray. Call on Him. His hope and
healing reach beyond this life into the next.

Tempered by Love

You are my God. Show me what you want me to do, and let your gentle Spirit lead me in the right path.

PSALM 143:10 CEV

God doesn't drag His children through life by the wrist like a domineering parent with a self-centered agenda. God leads with love, gently and quietly. God's Spirit whispers, "Go this way," as a verse of scripture crosses your mind. He tenderly nudges your conscience toward making good choices and reaching out in love. He brings comfort in countless creative ways that those who don't recognize Him label as coincidence. God's gentleness reminds us that His power is always tempered by love.

Leap of Faith

The LORD protects those
of childlike faith.

PSALM 116:6 NLT

Feel like you need more faith? Sometimes what we really need is the courage to act on what we already believe. A skydiver may have faith her parachute is packed correctly, but that doesn't stop her stomach from doing its own loop-de-loop as she jumps out of the plane. However, the more she dives, the less nervous she feels. The better you know God, the more a leap of faith feels like a hop into a loving Father's waiting arms.

Loss of a Pet

*Peace I leave with you, my peace I give
unto you: not as the world giveth, give I
unto you. Let not your heart be troubled,
neither let it be afraid.*

JOHN 14:27

My child's beloved dog died this morning,
Lord, and he is full of sorrow. Some mock
his tears, but his grief is very real to him. I
hug him close and offer words of comfort,
but that won't bring back his playmate.
Please fill the void in his life, and comfort
him in Your special way.

Call for Help

Cast your burden on the LORD, and He shall sustain you; He shall never permit the righteous to be moved.

PSALM 55:22 NKJV

Casting a fishing line is an almost effortless motion. Casting a burden paints a totally different image. Burdens are pictured as heavy, cumbersome, not easily carried—let alone "cast." But casting our burdens on God is as easy as speaking to Him in prayer. It's calling for help when we need it, admitting our sin when we've fallen, and letting our tears speak for our hearts when words fail us.

Love Like Jesus

God sets the lonely in families.
PSALM 68:6 NIV

Family can be one of our greatest joys in this life. It can also be messy, because it's where we show our true colors. It's where we're real. That's why "family" is the perfect petri dish for us to learn how to love like Jesus. Unconditional love sees others for who they really are, warts and all, and continues to reach out, sacrifice, and forgive. As we allow God to love us, He will help us more readily love others.

Forever Faithful

*The LORD is good. His unfailing love
continues forever, and his faithfulness
continues to each generation.*

PSALM 100:5 NLT

With time, we come to believe certain things are unshakable. The sun rises and sets. The tides ebb and flow. Seasons revolve year after year. Babies are born, people die, and the world goes on pretty much as it has for centuries: faithful to a predictable pattern. But there will come a time when the world as we know it will end. Only God is totally unshakable and unchanging. His love and goodness to us will remain forever faithful.

DAY 56

Doing Life Together

*I will always praise you in the
presence of your faithful people.*

PSALM 52:9 NIV

Fellowship is a fancy word for getting
together with others who love God. It's
more than going to church. It's doing life
together. Whether you're meeting as a small
group for Bible study or simply chatting
one-on-one over a cup of coffee about what
God is doing in your lives, you're experienc-
ing fellowship. When faith and friendship
come together with honesty and authentic-
ity, relationships thrive—between you and
God and between you and your spiritual
brothers and sisters.

Rescued!

For by grace are ye saved through faith;
and that not of yourselves:
it is the gift of God.

EPHESIANS 2:8

Salvation is something we all long for in one way or another, Father, and the salvation You've provided far surpasses anything that could be presented by mankind. You've rescued me from the depths of sin and given me new life in Christ, and I will ever praise You!

Managing Finances

*If your wealth increases, don't
make it the center of your life.*

PSALM 62:10 NLT

Money is an important tool. You can use it
to repair your car, pay your rent, or help put
food on the table. But it's just a tool. Loving
it would be like loving a socket wrench. It
can't love you back or change who you are.
It can only do its job. Ultimately, the true
value of a tool depends on how well you use
it. Allow God to show you how to wield your
finances wisely.

Absolute Acceptance

*But let me run loose and free,
celebrating GOD's great work,
every bone in my body laughing,
singing, "GOD, there's no one like you."*

PSALM 35:9 MSG

Knowing you're loved without condition sets you free. It invites you to abandon insecurity, relax, and enjoy being yourself. It encourages you to go ahead and try, because failure is simply a steep learning curve. God's acceptance of you is the key to this freedom. As you rest in God's absolute acceptance, you'll discover the confidence and courage you need to push beyond who you are today and become the woman you were created to be.

DAY 60

Beautiful Blossoms

*Your wife shall be like a fruitful
vine in the very heart of your house,
your children like olive plants
all around your table.*

PSALM 128:3 NKJV

There are many ways to be fruitful. One way
is through relationships. Whether it's with
family, friends, neighbors, church members,
or coworkers, the things you say and do can
be buds that blossom into something beautiful. Who will you spend time with today?
Each encounter is an opportunity to plant
a seed. Will it be a seed of encouragement,
grace, faith, comfort, or. . . ? Ask God to help
you know the type of seed others need.

A Wonderful Cycle

*Good will come to those who
are generous and lend freely,
who conduct their affairs with justice.*

PSALM 112:5 NIV

A funny thing happens when you get in the habit of sharing what God has given you. The more you give, the more you realize how blessed you are and the more grateful you become—which inspires you to share even more of what you have with others. It's a wonderful cycle that loosens your grip on material things so both your hands and your heart can more freely reach out to those around you.

Closer to God

*You have also given me the shield
of Your salvation; Your right hand
has held me up, Your gentleness
has made me great.*

PSALM 18:35 NKJV

A children's fable describes the sun and wind making a bet: Who can get a man to take off his coat? The wind blows with vengeance, using his strength to try and force the man's hand. The sun simply shines, gently inviting the man to shed what he no longer needs. God does the same with us. His gentleness warms us toward love and faith. The closer we draw to God, the more we'll treat others as He's treated us.

Let the Children Come

Verily I say unto you, Whosoever shall not receive the kingdom of God as a little child, he shall not enter therein.

MARK 10:15

You said that accepting You requires child-like faith, dear Jesus. Yet so often we fail to take the young ones seriously. We think they're too young to understand, but You said to let them come. Give us wisdom when dealing with the little ones, and help us encourage them to accept You as well.

DAY 64

Answers to Prayer

The humble will see their God at work and be glad. Let all who seek God's help be encouraged.

PSALM 69:32 NLT

There's encouragement in answered prayer. Sometimes God's answers look exactly like what we were hoping for. Other times they reveal that God's love, wisdom, and creativity far surpass ours. To be aware of God's answers to prayer, we have to keep our eyes and hearts open. Be on the alert for answers to prayer today. When you catch sight of one, thank God. Allow the assurance of God's everlasting care to encourage your soul.

Your Deepest Longings

*All my longings lie open
before you, Lord; my sighing
is not hidden from you.*

PSALM 38:9 NIV

What does your heart long for most? Talk to God about it. He'll help you uncover the true root of your deepest desires. Longing for a child? Perhaps what you're really longing for is unconditional love. Longing for a home of your own? Perhaps it's your need for security or to be admired by others that you crave. Ultimately, God is the only one who can fill your deepest longings—and it's His desire to do exactly that.

A Good Life

*"Only you are my Lord! Every good
thing I have is a gift from you."*

PSALM 16:2 CEV

What is good about your life? Consider how
every good thing we receive can be tied
back to God. Family. Friends. Talents. The
ability to earn an income. It's easy to take
the good things in our lives for granted,
while readily putting the blame on God when
we feel things go wrong. The next time you
notice you're feeling happy about something
good in your life, look for the part God played
in sending it your way.

The Quiet Side of Love

With all my heart I praise the LORD!
I will never forget how kind he has been.

PSALM 103:2 CEV

Kindness is a quiet side of love. It isn't showy, demanding center stage. It often serves in the background meeting needs, offering a word of encouragement or an impromptu hug. Sometimes kindness even travels under the name "anonymous." Likewise, the kindnesses God showers upon our lives often fall into the anonymous category. They're the coincidences, the unexpected pleasures, the little things that lift our hearts during a difficult day. How has God's kindness enriched your life this week?

Prepare Your Heart

I will instruct you and teach you in the way you should go; I will counsel you with my loving eye on you.

PSALM 32:8 NIV

To learn, you have to listen. Are you really listening to what God is trying to teach you? Whether it's reading the Bible, listening to a message at church, or receiving counsel from someone who is farther down the road of faith than you happen to be, there is always more to learn. Prepare your heart with prayer. Ask God to help you clearly understand what you need to learn, and then act on what you hear.

A Life That Honors God

*Teach us to use wisely
all the time we have.*

PSALM 90:12 CEV

Want to live life in a way that honors God? There are so many options that it's hard to know what to do. But in Matthew 22:37–39, Jesus sums up the purpose of life by saying we're to love God and love others. Prayerfully weighing the choices before us against these two commands can help us make wise decisions. We don't know how long our lives will be, but with love as our goal, we're certain to use our time well.

The Greatest of Miracles

And we know that the Son of
God is come, and hath given us an
understanding, that we may know him
that is true; and we are in him that is
true, even in his Son Jesus Christ.
This is the true God, and eternal life.

1 JOHN 5:20

We are such a frenetic lot, dear God, but when we get all worked up, You say, "Stand still." You offer complete salvation but only when we take the time to see from where our deliverance comes. Help us slow down and witness the greatest of miracles.

Returning Love

*As high as the heavens are above
the earth, so great is his love
for those who fear him.*

PSALM 103:11 NIV

It's hard to grasp how deeply God cares for us, because our firsthand experience of love comes from relationships with imperfect people. But God's love is different. With God, we need never fear condemnation, misunderstanding, or rejection. He completely understands what we say and how we feel—and loves us without condition. Since God is never fickle or self-centered, we can risk opening up every part of our lives to Him. We can risk returning the love He so freely gives.

Hope for Redemption

*Surely goodness and mercy shall follow
me all the days of my life; and I will
dwell in the house of the LORD forever.*

PSALM 23:6 NKJV

In old-fashioned melodramas and classic films, repentant scoundrels throw themselves on the mercy of the court. This means they know what they've done is wrong, there's no possible way they can make it right, and their only hope for redemption is to ask the court to extend what they don't deserve: mercy. God extends mercy to us each day. He's sentenced us to life—eternal life—and to the freedom to grow in the shelter of His love.

A Patient Perspective

Be patient and trust the LORD.
Don't let it bother you when all goes
well for those who do sinful things.

PSALM 37:7 CEV

When we encounter conflict or injustice, we want resolution. We want relationships to be mended and wrongs to be made right. We want villains to pay and victims to heal. Now. Wanting this life to resemble heaven is a God-given desire. But the fact is, we're not home yet. If you're impatient for a situation to change, pray for perspective, do what you can, and then trust God for resolution in His time and in His way.

Peace of Heart

Let them continually say,
"Great is the LORD, who delights
in blessing his servant with peace!"

PSALM 35:27 NLT

The peace God pours out on those who follow Him runs deeper than peace of mind. It overflows into peace of heart. As you trust God a little more each day, placing the things you cherish most in His loving hands, you will release a need to control, a tendency toward worry, and a fear for the future. In their place, you will discover the comfort of being cared for like a child being held in a parent's nurturing embrace.

In His Image

*Be of the same mind one toward
another. Mind not high things,
but condescend to men of low estate.
Be not wise in your own conceits.*

ROMANS 12:16

There's such a fine line between self-esteem and arrogance. Sometimes I have trouble distinguishing between the two. Father, You created me in Your image. For that I am thankful, but I need to remember that I'm not perfect. Help me not to be proud but to daily strive to be more like You.

The Brilliance of Blessing

Let your conversation be without covetousness; and be content with such things as ye have: for he hath said, I will never leave thee, nor forsake thee.

HEBREWS 13:5

You've promised to walk with me all the way and provide all that I need, dear God, and I'm rejoicing in that guarantee. What more do I need? It doesn't matter that the world presents shiny trinkets. Their luster dims in the brilliance of the blessings and contentment that You give.

Opportunities for Encouragement

*Anxiety weighs down the heart,
but a kind word cheers it up.*

PROVERBS 12:25 NIV

You gave me an amazing opportunity today, Father, and it's all a result of a discouraging situation. You helped me as I struggled through the problem, and because of that I was able to encourage someone else who faced a similar difficulty. You really are an awesome God!

Worthy

*You make your saving help my shield,
and your right hand sustains me;
your help has made me great.*

PSALM 18:35 NIV

Accomplishing something worthwhile is one of the joys of living. It can give you a sense of purpose and worth. But you are more than the sum of your accomplishments. You are an accomplished woman simply by continuing to mature into the individual God created you to be. Enjoy using every gift, talent, and ability God has so generously woven into you while resting in the fact that you are worthy of God's love, regardless of what you've achieved.

God's Love Letter

Every word you give me is a miracle word—how could I help but obey? Break open your words, let the light shine out, let ordinary people see the meaning.

PSALM 119:129 MSG

The Bible isn't a novel to be read for entertainment, a textbook to be skimmed for knowledge, a manual for living, or a collection of inspirational sayings. The Bible is a love letter. It's the story of God's love for His children from the beginning of the world until the end—and beyond. It's a book that takes time to know well, but God promises His own Spirit will help us understand what we read. All we need to do is ask.

When You're Hurting

*But the God of all grace, who hath
called us unto his eternal glory
by Christ Jesus, after that ye have
suffered a while, make you perfect,
stablish, strengthen, settle you.*

I PETER 5:10

It's so hard to express grief in our society, Jesus, but I'm glad You don't reject us when we do. After all, You grieved, and You showed me how to handle perhaps one of the deepest human emotions. Thank You for letting me come to You when I'm hurting. Thank You for Your love.

God's Design

*I am lonely and troubled. Show that you
care and have pity on me.*

PSALM 25:16 CEV

In Genesis we read about creation. God
declared everything He created "good," with
one exception. God said it was not good for
Adam to be alone. God designed people to
be in relationships with each other and with
Him. When you're feeling lonely, God agrees:
It's not good. Ask God to bring a new friend
your way and help you connect more deeply
with those already in your life. But for right
now, invite God to meet your deepest need.

His Power at Work

My power and my strength come from the LORD, and he has saved me.

PSALM 118:14 CEV

Moses parted the Red Sea. Peter walked upon the waves. David slaughtered a giant with a single stone. God's power was the force behind them all. How will God's power work through you? Perhaps you'll conquer an addiction, face your fear of public speaking, forgive what seems unforgivable, serve the homeless, or lead someone into a closer relationship with God. When God is honored through what you do, you can be sure His power is at work in you.

He Is Near

The LORD is near to all who call on him,
to all who call on him in truth.

PSALM 145:18 NIV

Some mornings you wake up with the knowledge that a challenging day is ahead of you. Other times, difficulty catches you by surprise. Whatever challenge enters your life, remind yourself that the Lord is near. Not only will God help you meet each challenge head-on, but He will also use each one to help you grow. Look for God's hand at work in your life, helping you achieve what may seem impossible.

Reason for Praise

*Better is one day in your courts
than a thousand elsewhere.*

PSALM 84:10 NIV

What words would you use to describe God?
Loving. Forgiving. Powerful. Creative. Wise.
Merciful. Eternal. Glorious. Dependable.
Truthful. Compassionate. Faithful. Friend.
Father. Savior. Every word you can think of is
reason for praise. When you pray, share more
than a list of requests with God. Tell God how
much He means to you. Choose one attribute
of God and tell Him how that character trait
has made a difference in your life.

You Are Special

*You made all the delicate,
inner parts of my body and knit
me together in my mother's womb.*

PSALM 139:13 NLT

How can I doubt my worth in Your eyes,
Father? You know the number of hairs on my
head. You created me, and You said that Your
creation is very good. When I'm tempted to
get down on myself, remind me that I am special to You, and there's no one just like me.

Eternal Choice

*My choice is you, GOD, first and only.
And now I find I'm your choice!*
PSALM 16:5 MSG

Some choices we make change the course
of our lives, such as whether we'll remain
single or marry, what career we'll pursue,
whether or not to adopt a child. But there's
one choice that changes not only the direction of our lives, but also our eternity. When
we choose to follow God, it affects every
choice we make from that moment forward.
The more we involve God in our decision
process, the wiser our choices will be.

Eternal Commitment

He always stands by his covenant—
the commitment he made to
a thousand generations.

PSALM 105:8 NLT

God has made a commitment to you similar to a wedding vow. He promises to love and cherish you through sickness and health, prosperity or poverty, good times and bad. But with God, this commitment doesn't last until "death do you part." Even in death and beyond, God is there. There's nothing you can do that will make Him turn His face from you. His commitment to love and forgive you stands steadfast, come what may.

In His Hands

Those who are righteous will be long remembered. They do not fear bad news; they confidently trust the LORD to care for them. They are confident and fearless and can face their foes triumphantly.

PSALM 112:6–8 NLT

We live in uncertain times, economically, politically, and globally. Yet you can greet each new day with your head held high, confident and unafraid. Why? Because you have a God who cares deeply about you and the world around you. When your confidence is placed firmly in God instead of your own abilities, bank account, or "good karma," you need not fear the future. It's in God's powerful, capable, and compassionate hands.

Saved to Serve

*If a man therefore purge himself from
these, he shall be a vessel unto honour,
sanctified, and meet for the master's
use, and prepared unto every good work.*

2 TIMOTHY 2:21

I'm not sure how many times I've heard the
saying "God saved me to serve, not to sit."
There are so many ways I can be involved
in Christian service. What I need most is a
willing heart. Help me never to lose sight of
the fact that servanthood is beautiful in Your
sight and a blessing to others.

True Courage

*Wait on the LORD; be of good courage,
and He shall strengthen your heart;
wait, I say, on the LORD!*

PSALM 27:14 NKJV

Foolhardiness can look like courage at first glance. However, true courage counts the cost before it forges ahead. If you're faced with a risky decision, it's not only wise to think before you act but also biblical. Ecclesiastes 3:1 (MSG) reminds us, "There's an opportune time to do things, a right time for everything on the earth." Waiting for that right time takes patience and courage. Don't simply pray for courage. Pray for the wisdom to discern that "opportune time."

A Clean Slate

*Clean the slate, God, so we can
start the day fresh! Keep me from
stupid sins, from thinking I can
take over your work.*

PSALM 19:13 MSG

Yesterday is over. Today is a brand-new day. Any mistakes or bad choices you've made in the past are behind you. God doesn't hold them against you. He's wiped your past clean with the power of forgiveness. The only thing left for you to do with the past is learn from it. Celebrate each new day by giving thanks to God for what He's done and actively anticipating what He's going to do with the clean slate of today.

DAY 92

Wise Decisions

I say to GOD, "Be my Lord!"
Without you, nothing makes sense.
PSALM 16:2 MSG

Paper or plastic. Right or left. Yes or no. Every day is filled with decisions that need to be made. Some have little bearing on the big picture of our lives, while others can change its course in dramatic ways. Inviting God into our decision-making process not only is wise, but also helps us find peace with the decisions we make. Knowing God is at work, weaving all our decisions into a life of purpose, helps us move forward with confidence.

Simple Blessings

*It is of the LORD's mercies that we are
not consumed, because his compassions
fail not. They are new every morning:
great is thy faithfulness.*

LAMENTATIONS 3:22–23

Thank You for the many happy times
You've given me. So often it's the little
things in life—the first robin in the spring,
the first homegrown tomato of the season,
even a brilliant sunset. These simple blessings evoke the biggest smiles and make me
the happiest!

He Delights in You

Take delight in the LORD, and he will give you the desires of your heart.

PSALM 37:4 NIV

To "delight" in someone is to take great pleasure from simply being in that person's presence. If you truly delight in God, the deepest desire of your heart will be to draw ever closer to Him. This is a desire God Himself delights in filling. That's because God delights in you. You are more than His creation. You are His beloved child. He delights in you like a proud father watching his daughter take her very first steps.

A Free Gift

*I'll bless you every day, and keep
it up from now to eternity.*

PSALM 145:2 MSG

Eternal life isn't a reward we can earn. It's
a free gift given by a Father who wants to
spend eternity with the children He loves.
This gift may be free to us, but it was purchased at a high price. Jesus purchased our
lives at the cost of His own. His death on the
cross is the bridge that leads us from this
life into the next. Forever isn't long to say
thank you for a gift like that.

DAY 96

The Ultimate Example

*I will study your teachings
and follow your footsteps.*

PSALM 119:15 CEV

In the Bible we read about heroes like
Abraham, Moses, and David. Though these
men did admirable things, they were also
flawed. They made mistakes and poor
choices. Nevertheless, God used them in re-
markable ways. The only person in the Bible
who lived a perfect life was Jesus. He is our
ultimate example. If you're searching for the
best way to live and love, Jesus' footsteps are
the only ones wholly worth following.

A Faith Workout

Lead me by your truth and teach me,
for you are the God who saves me.
All day long I put my hope in you.
PSALM 25:5 NLT

Faith is both a gift we receive and an action we take. God's Spirit gives us enough faith to reach out to a Father we cannot see. But as we continue reaching—continue putting our trust in God as we go through life—that little gift of faith grows stronger, like a muscle consistently put to work at the gym. Give your faith a workout today by doing what you believe God wants you to do.

For His Glory

But you are a chosen generation, a royal priesthood, a holy nation, His own special people, that you may proclaim the praises of Him who called you out of darkness into His marvelous light.

I PETER 2:9 NKJV

Stress seems so overrated these days, doesn't it, Lord? Every time I turn around someone is telling me how stressed they are. And I do the same thing. I guess it's popular to be stressed. Popular maybe—but not good. Please take my stress and turn it into energy that is used for Your glory.

Difficult Days

Stay with GOD! Take heart. Don't quit.
I'll say it again: Stay with GOD.
PSALM 27:14 MSG

Life is short, but some days seem to last forever. When you're facing a difficult day, don't face it alone. Take a good look at your exhaustion, anxiety, and fears. Picture entrusting them, one by one, into God's hands. Then take an objective look at what you need to do today. Invite God to join you as you take one step at a time in accomplishing what lies ahead. Throughout the day, remind yourself that God is right by your side.

An Accurate Measure

*When doubts filled my mind,
your comfort gave me
renewed hope and cheer.*

PSALM 94:19 NLT

What are your emotions telling you today? You're unloved? Insignificant? A failure? Powerless to change? What you feel is not always an accurate measure of what is real. When your emotions try to take you on a roller-coaster ride, refuse to buckle yourself in. Ask God to help you sort through what's going on in your mind and heart. Cling to what God says is true, not to what your fickle emotions whisper on a poor self-image day.

DAY 101

Nothing Remains

*As far as the east is from the west,
so far has he removed our
transgressions from us.*

PSALM 103:12 NIV

Picture a chalkboard. Written on it is everything you've ever done that goes against what
God has asked of you. What would you see
written there? How big would the chalkboard
be? Now imagine God wiping it clean with
one swipe of His hand. Nothing remains, not
the faintest image of one single word. That's
how completely God has forgiven you. When
guilt or shame over past mistakes threatens
to creep back into your life, remember the
empty chalkboard—and rejoice.

Share It!

*You have helped me, and I sing happy
songs in the shadow of your wings.*

PSALM 63:7 CEV

Happiness can be contagious. Why not
spread some of yours around? Consider the
ways God helps you nurture a happy heart.
How has He comforted you, encouraged you,
strengthened you? If you're happy, share
it. Tell someone close to you what God has
done. Smile warmly at those who cross your
path. Surprise someone with a gift just because. Express to God how you feel in song.
Thank God for the little things—such as the
ability to feel happy.

Incorruptible Beauty

*Charm is deceptive, and beauty does
not last; but a woman who fears the
LORD will be greatly praised.*

PROVERBS 31:30 NLT

I was glancing through a magazine today, and there were so many tips on being beautiful. As I looked at the models, I thought about how few people really look like that. And I realized something like a car crash could change it all instantly. Inner beauty isn't like that, is it, Father? It's from You, and it's incorruptible.

Don't Wait

*Open up before GOD,
keep nothing back; he'll do
whatever needs to be done.*

PSALM 37:5 MSG

You can't keep a secret from God. He knows you inside and out. That doesn't mean you can't hold out on Him. There may be things you'd rather not discuss: areas of shame, bitterness, or rebellion. He'll never muscle His way into those parts of your heart. He's waiting for an invitation. If you're honest about wanting real change in your life, don't wait any longer. Open up before God. Grace, forgiveness, and healing are yours for the asking.

As God Sees

Though the LORD is great,
he cares for the humble, but he
keeps his distance from the proud.
PSALM 138:6 NLT

Beloved child, rebellious daughter; faithful friend, self-centered competitor; fully forgiven, fickle and flawed; priceless miracle, nothing but dust: You are the sum of all of these things and more. Acknowledging that you're a crazy quilt of weakness and strength is a step toward humility. After all, true humility isn't regarding yourself as less significant than others. It's seeing yourself the way God does, as no more or less than you truly are.

A Full Life

Joyful are people of integrity, who follow the instructions of the LORD.

PSALM 119:1 NLT

Modern culture tells us that "bad girls" have all the fun. Don't believe it. A self-centered life is an empty life. When you choose to follow God and live a life of integrity, regret no longer knocks at your door. In its place you find joy. There are no worries about your past catching up with you or some half-truth being exposed. You're ready to live life to the fullest, a life in which love and respect are freely given and received.

The Source of Happiness

Happy is that people, that is in such a case: yea, happy is that people, whose God is the LORD.

PSALM 144:15

I'm glad money isn't required to obtain true happiness, or I wouldn't get much. You meet my needs sufficiently, but the happiness I enjoy when I'm with family or just relaxing with a good book on a lazy afternoon is beyond sufficient. True happiness really can't be bought, can it, Jesus?

Going the Distance

*The godly offer good counsel;
they teach right from wrong.*

PSALM 37:30 NLT

Want to run a marathon? Talk to those who've run one before. They know how to train, which shoes to buy, and what to expect when the big day arrives. The same is true if you want to go the distance with God. When you meet people who have followed God for many years, ask questions. Discover what they've learned, where they've struggled, and how they study the Bible. You may gain new friends, as well as godly counsel.

Aware of His Presence

I can always count on you—
God, my dependable love.

PSALM 59:17 MSG

When you're feeling lonely, picture God beside you in the room. Talk to Him the way you would a dear friend. If praying aloud feels awkward, journal or write God a love note that you can tuck in your Bible. Read the book of Psalms. See what other people had to say to God when they felt the way you do right now. Remember, God is with you, whether you're aware of His presence or not.

God's Artwork

He determines the number of the stars and calls them each by name.

PSALM 147:4 NIV

Like a child who carefully chooses the silver crayon to draw the dog with stars for eyes, God's artwork is an expression of who He is. It displays His creativity, attention to detail, love of diversity, meticulous organization, and even His sense of humor. Taking time to contemplate the beauty and complexity of nature can help paint a clearer picture for you of what God is like. He's an artist, as well as a Father, Savior, and friend.

Following God's Lead

*Love and faithfulness meet
together; righteousness and
peace kiss each other.*

PSALM 85:10 NIV

When you follow God's lead and do what you know He wants you to do, you discover a place of peace. Outward struggles may continue, but inside you can relax. You've done what you could with what God has given you—and that's enough. Listen for God's whisper of, "Well done, my beautiful daughter." It's there. Rest in that place of peace, and allow yourself to celebrate how far you've come and to anticipate what is still ahead.

Prayer

I've thrown myself headlong into your arms—I'm celebrating your rescue. I'm singing at the top of my lungs, I'm so full of answered prayers.

PSALM 13:5–6 MSG

When we pray, we expect things to happen—and they do. Inviting the Creator of the universe to be intimately involved in the details of our day is a mysterious and miraculous undertaking. But prayer isn't a tool. It's a conversation. God is not our almighty personal planner, helping us manage our lives more efficiently. He's Someone who loves us. When you pray, remember you're speaking to Someone who enjoys you, as well as takes care of you.

True Beauty

*Do not let your adornment be merely
outward—arranging the hair, wearing gold,
or putting on fine apparel—
rather let it be the hidden person of
the heart, with the incorruptible beauty
of a gentle and quiet spirit, which is very
precious in the sight of God.*

1 PETER 3:3–4 NKJV

I saw the prettiest child at the park today,
Father. Her beautiful smile reached her eyes.
I think it must have reached her heart, too,
because I also saw this little girl go right up and
play with a child who had a disability—a child
whom other kids were teasing. Lord, thank
You for showing me what inner beauty is.

Angels of Protection

*The angel of the LORD encamps
around those who fear him,
and he delivers them.*

PSALM 34:7 NIV

In the Bible we read about angelic beings
who act as God's messengers and warriors.
Far from cute little cherubs who do nothing more than pluck harps on cotton ball
clouds, we meet angels who yield swords
and have ferocious lionlike faces. But the
message they continually tell God's children
is, "Be not afraid." When you're in need of
protection, remember there's more going
on than is visible to the eye. God's angels
have your back.

Because of Who He Is. . .

My soul thirsts for God, for the living God. When can I go and meet with God?

PSALM 42:2 NIV

When you're in love, you long to be with the one who has captured your heart. It makes little difference if you're sharing a sumptuous sunset dinner cruise or toiling together to complete a mundane task. What matters is that you're together. When we first get to know God, we long to spend time with Him because of what He provides. But the longer we spend in His presence, the more we desire Him simply because of who He is.

What Do You Need?

*Each day that we live, he provides
for our needs and gives us the
strength of a young eagle.*

PSALM 103:5 CEV

What do you need today? Whether it's the finances to pay a fast-approaching bill or the courage to have a difficult conversation with a friend, God wants to provide what you need. Share your heart with Him. But before you rush off to other things, sit quietly and listen. God may reveal how you can work with Him to meet that need. He may also want to help you share with others what He's already so generously provided.

Beautiful!

You are altogether beautiful.
SONG OF SOLOMON 4:7 NIV

Yesterday I heard a little boy ask his
mother why she was purchasing cosmet-
ics. "To help me look better," was her reply.
"But you're beautiful," the boy said with
conviction. The mother smiled brightly
and gave the child a hug. As he returned the
embrace, the love between them was unmis-
takable. Lord, at that moment I knew—she
was beautiful!

Ritual vs. Relationship

Keep company with GOD,
get in on the best.

PSALM 37:4 MSG

Sometimes, drawing close to God can feel like an eternal to-do list instead of a relationship. If praying, reading scripture, going to church, or serving others begins to feel like just another task, don't settle for checking them off your list. That's ritual, not relationship. Instead, make a date with God. Set up a time and place. Then simply talk and listen. Focus on who God is. Take the time to fall in love with Him all over again.

A Good Parent

*I will instruct you and teach you
in the way you should go; I will
guide you with My eye.*

PSALM 32:8 NKJV

From the time I was a child, one of my greatest dreams was to be a mother. I did pretty well when I pretended with my dolls, but reality is a lot different. Now that I have children, I'm not always so sure of myself. Please, God, give me wisdom and courage to be a good parent.

A Good Steward

*Do you not know that your bodies
are temples of the Holy Spirit, who
is in you, whom you have received from
God? You are not your own;
you were bought at a price.
Therefore honor God with your bodies.*

1 CORINTHIANS 6:19–20 NIV

Sometimes I get pretty confused, Lord. I try to eat right, exercise properly, and get plenty of rest, but all of the "experts" say different things about what I should be doing. It's important that I am a good steward of the body You've given me, so please help me to care for myself the right way.

Refreshed!

Weeping may stay for the night,
but rejoicing comes in the morning.

PSALM 30:5 NIV

Renewal isn't taking a deep breath, smiling through gritted teeth, and muscling your way through today. Renewal is a kind of rebirth. It's letting the past fall from your shoulders and welcoming hope back into your heart. Renewal is a work of the Spirit, not a state of mind or act of the will. It's joining hands with God and moving forward together, expectant and refreshed. Are you ready to release whatever's holding you back and reach out to God?

More Than a BFF

*But I, by your great love, can come
into your house; in reverence I bow
down toward your holy temple.*

PSALM 5:7 NIV

It's true God is our Friend. But He's more
than our BFF (Best Friend Forever). God is
our sovereign Lord and King. He's the One
who initiated this implausibly intimate relationship, Creator with creation. But God's
overwhelming love for us should not lull us
into a familiarity that disregards reverence
and respect. There will come a time when
every knee will bow to Him. Until that day,
may our awe and esteem continue to grow
right along with our love.

Motivated by Love

*My sacrifice, O God, is a broken spirit;
a broken and contrite heart, you,
God, will not despise.*

PSALM 51:17 NIV

Sacrifice can be motivated by love, necessity, or obligation. God asks only for sacrifices motivated by our love for Him. That doesn't mean they don't come at a price. When we place our own pride on the altar and acknowledge that God is in control and we are not, it can be painful. But it's like the pain that follows a much-needed surgery. It's a precursor to healing. What we give up out of love, we're better off without.

Look to the Son

Satisfy us each morning with your unfailing love, so we may sing for joy to the end of our lives.

PSALM 90:14 NLT

Each morning when you rise, take time to turn your eyes toward the Son. Take a fresh look at what Jesus has done out of love for you. Recall what you've been forgiven and the many blessings you've received. Consider how following in Jesus' footsteps has changed the direction of your life—and will change the day ahead. Allow gratitude to wash over you anew. There's no greater satisfaction than seeing your life in the light of God's great love.

God's Wisdom

For the LORD gives wisdom;
from His mouth come knowledge
and understanding.

PROVERBS 2:6 NKJV

I'm so forgetful! God, I know how many
times You've admonished me to seek Your
wisdom, yet over and over I try to do things
on my own. You'd think I would learn after
so many mistakes, but I guess I'm too proud.
I don't want to continue like this. I want
Your wisdom so that I can live life as You
intended.

Safe and Secure

The Lord is truthful; he can be trusted.
PSALM 33:4 CEV

God's power is limitless. That's tough to comprehend. But knowing God has the ability to care for us in any and all circumstances is not the true reason why we can feel safe and secure in His presence. Being in the presence of a beefy bodyguard only feels safe if you know that person is trustworthy, if you know he's on your side. God is on your side, fighting for you. You can trust His strength and His love.

A Desire to Serve

*Make my heart glad! I serve you,
and my prayer is sincere.*

PSALM 86:4 CEV

The people we love, we serve. If a friend's car breaks down, we give her a lift. If she's ill, we make her family a meal. We may use the word help instead of serve, but the result is the same. Love leads us to act. As our love for God grows, so will our desire to serve Him. One way we serve God is to care for those He loves. Ask God whom He'd like you to serve today.

Extension of Righteousness

Your righteousness is like the mighty mountains, your justice like the ocean depths. You care for people and animals alike, O LORD.

PSALM 36:6 NLT

God's goodness is more than Him playing "nice." God's goodness is an extension of His righteousness. Since God is loving and just, the morally virtuous thing for Him to do is provide His children with a balance of mercy and discipline, guidelines and grace. That's why a price had to be paid for our sins. God's righteousness demanded it. But God's love allowed Jesus to pay a debt we couldn't afford to pay on our own.

Sufficient Grace

*"My grace is sufficient for you, for My
strength is made perfect in weakness."
Therefore most gladly I will rather
boast in my infirmities, that the
power of Christ may rest upon me.*

2 CORINTHIANS 12:9 NKJV

I've been facing a physical difficulty
lately, and it seems to be getting worse.
I've prayed, dear God. Oh, how I've prayed.
Sometimes it feels like You are so far away,
but I know You are right here next to me
offering Your sufficient grace and strength.
Help me to accept this as Your answer.

What Matters

*I think about you before I go
to sleep, and my thoughts
turn to you during the night.*

PSALM 63:6 CEV

Close your day in a wonderful way by spending it in your Father's arms. Instead of allowing your thoughts to race ahead toward tomorrow, take time to savor today. Regardless of whether it's been a day you'll long remember or one you'd rather forget, ask God to help you recall what matters. Thank Him for His loving care. Ask forgiveness for any moments when you turned your back on Him. Then relax and rest, knowing He's near.

The Right Words

*May these words of my mouth and
this meditation of my heart be
pleasing in your sight, LORD,
my Rock and my Redeemer.*

PSALM 19:14 NIV

God hears the words you speak. He even hears the ones that remain unsaid anywhere other than your mind. Sometimes it's hard to get words past your lips. It's difficult to apologize, comfort someone who's hurting, or try to untangle miscommunication in a relationship. It can even be difficult to say, "I love you." With God's help, you can say what needs to be said. Ask God to help you speak the right words at the right time.

Seasons

"Be still, and know that I am God."
PSALM 46:10 NIV

What season of spiritual growth are you in? Springtime's early bud of new love? Basking in summer's sunshine, growing by fruitful leaps and bounds? Knee-deep in autumn, with remnants of your old life falling like dead leaves around your feet? Or praying your way through winter, where God and that joy of first love seem far away? Whatever season you're in, remember: God's the only One who can make something grow. Trust His timing and watch for fruit.

God-Honoring Opportunities

Give unto the LORD the glory due to His name; worship the LORD in the beauty of holiness.

PSALM 29:2 NKJV

There are many ways to be involved in my community, Father, and I ask You to show me what to do. I want to choose the activities that will help others and that will bring glory to You. Help me to weigh the possibilities carefully and to make the best decisions. Thank You for these opportunities to honor You.

Enjoyable Work

Tell God what you need,
and thank him for all he has done.

PHILIPPIANS 4:6 NLT

I'm blessed to have a job I enjoy, Lord. So many people aren't able to say the same, and many of them probably have good reason to dislike their work. Thank You for opening this door of opportunity for me. You've met my needs in a wonderful way.

The "Perfect" Prayer

The LORD has heard my cry for mercy;
the LORD accepts my prayer.

PSALM 6:9 NIV

People talk about "accepting" God into their lives. But it's God's acceptance of us that makes this possible. Because Jesus gave His life to pay the price for all the wrongs we've ever done, our perfect God can accept us wholeheartedly, even though we're far from perfect people. God not only accepts us but also accepts our imperfect prayers. We don't have to worry about saying just the right words. The "perfect" prayer is simply sharing what's on our hearts.

Your Coworker

*Unless the LORD builds the house,
the builders labor in vain.*

PSALM 127:1 NIV

We were designed to do great things hand in hand with a very great God. So why not invite God to be your coworker in every endeavor you undertake today? Call on Him throughout the day, anytime you need wisdom, peace, or perseverance. Allow God to infuse you with creativity, humility, and compassion, regardless of the size of the task at hand. Your hard work, guided by prayer and undergirded by the Spirit of a mighty God, can accomplish amazing things.

No Greater Assurance

*The LORD will work out his plans for
my life—for your faithful love,
O LORD, endures forever.*

PSALM 138:8 NLT

Throughout scripture, God continually
reassures us that He's working on our
behalf to accomplish the good things He
has planned for our lives. If your confidence
wavers, if you need to know for certain someone is on your side, if you're anxious about
the future, do what people who've felt the very
same way have done for centuries: Take God's
words to heart. There's no greater assurance
than knowing you're loved, completely and
eternally.

Do-Overs

GOD made my life complete when I
placed all the pieces before him.
When I got my act together,
he gave me a fresh start.

PSALM 18:20 MSG

Picture your life as a jigsaw puzzle. You've been trying to put it together for years, with limited success. Some pieces are lost or bent beyond recognition. What's worse is that you have no idea what the final picture is supposed to be. Want a do-over? God offers you one. Simply admit you need His help. Then hand the pieces of your life over to Him. God will help you create a life that's beautiful, significant, and complete.

God's Loving Touch

*Is anyone among you suffering?
Let him pray. Is anyone cheerful?
Let him sing psalms. Is anyone
among you sick? Let him call for
the elders of the church, and let
them pray over him, anointing him
with oil in the name of the Lord.
And the prayer of faith will save the
sick, and the Lord will raise him up.*

JAMES 5:13–15 NKJV

You brought healing to so many people in the Bible, Jesus. Those were exciting times for those individuals, and it's still a spectacular miracle when You make someone whole today. Thank You for the many times You've touched my sick body or brought relief to my loved ones. Your loving touch produces great joy.

DAY 140

Your Personal Trainer

*Pile your troubles on God's shoulders—
he'll carry your load, he'll help you out.*
PSALM 55:22 MSG

You can gain physical strength by heading to the gym. However, spiritual strength is what you need to carry you through life. Instead of lifting weights, lift your eyes and prayers toward heaven. Stretch your compassion by reaching out to those around you in love. Get your heart pumping as you push beyond your own limitations and rely more completely on God. Through it all, God will be your strength as well as your personal trainer.

God's Blessing

*May he grant your heart's desires and
make all your plans succeed.*

PSALM 20:4 NLT

It's tempting to do what we want—while asking God to bless what we do. But a "please bless my efforts" prayer is not a rubber stamp of God's approval or our success. Regardless of what's on your agenda today, invite God to be part of your plans—from the conception stage right through to the celebration of its completion. God will help you align your motives and methods with His own and succeed in the ways that matter most.

Thank Him Today

*What a beautiful thing, GOD, to give
thanks, to sing an anthem to you,
the High God! To announce your love
each daybreak, sing your faithful
presence all through the night.*

PSALM 92:1 MSG

It used to be considered proper etiquette to send a handwritten thank-you note for every gift you received. Consider how high a stack of note cards you'd need if you formally thanked God for every gift He's given. Sending a thank-you via prayer or singing God's praises are the most common ways God's children express their gratitude to Him. But don't let that stop you from getting creative.

What new way can you thank God today?

Almighty God

*Sing to him, sing praise to him;
tell of all his wonderful acts.*

1 CHRONICLES 16:9 NIV

We all like to be praised—especially when it comes from those we love, or those we go the extra mile for. God likes to hear our praise as well. Although He can see that we appreciate the blessings He pours out on our lives, He still likes to hear us speak the words. We should pause often to praise God for the mighty things He's done for us, for His presence in our lives, and the hope we have for the future.

Step Out in Faith

Some trust in chariots and some in horses, but we trust in the name of the LORD our God.

PSALM 20:7 NIV

In the United States our currency proclaims, "In God We Trust." That's easier said than done. It can be tempting to trust more in the money this motto is printed on than in God Himself. That's because trusting God means trusting someone we cannot see. It's like trusting an invisible chair to hold your weight. You may believe it's there, but actually sitting down takes faith. When your trust wavers, recall God's faithfulness to you. Then step out in faith—and sit.

What Do You Think About?

You have tested my thoughts and examined my heart in the night. You have scrutinized me and found nothing wrong.

PSALM 17:3 NLT

When your mind wanders, where does it go? In your most unguarded moments, when you're no longer focused on deadlines and demands, what you think about is a strong indicator of what matters most to you. Pay attention to where your train of thought leads. Is it a direction you really want to go? If you find your mind traveling roads that draw you away from God, set your thoughts back on track toward what's truly worth focusing on.

Where the Heart Is

*And I will give them an heart to know
me, that I am the LORD: and they shall
be my people, and I will be their God:
for they shall return unto me
with their whole heart.*

JEREMIAH 24:7

I've heard it said that home is where the
heart is, and I suppose there's a lot of truth
in that. My home is such a special place, and
it seems that often when I'm somewhere
else, I am longing to be back in that place,
surrounded by what is comfortable and
familiar. Thank You, Father, for that opportunity to return home.

God's Truth

*Unspoken truth is
spoken everywhere.*

PSALM 19:4 MSG

God's truth is made known through the Bible. But it's also proclaimed throughout all of His creation. The seasons speak of God's faithfulness. The night sky sings of His glory. Thunderstorms shout of His might. And the first heartbeat of each child whispers, "Yes, God still performs miracles." Listen for God's truth as you go through your day. Take what you hear and compare it with what you read in God's Word. God's truth isn't concealed. It's revealed every day.

Every Corner

Keep your eye on the healthy soul,
scrutinize the straight life; there's
a future in strenuous wholeness.

PSALM 37:37 MSG

The word holistic is often linked with medicine. It describes an approach to treatment that addresses the whole person instead of just the physical symptoms. If you read the Gospels, you'll see this is how Jesus cared for people. He met their physical, mental, and emotional needs as well as their spiritual ones. It's not only your eternity that matters to God; it's your here and now. Invite God into every corner of your life.

He cares about them all.

Intentionality

*Teach us to number our days,
that we may gain a heart of wisdom.*

PSALM 90:12 NIV

Our days are numbered. That isn't a warning. It's a promise. Nothing can cut our lives short of what God has ordained for each one of us to live. Living life in light of our mortality isn't a morose pastime. It's a mind-set that can help us make wise choices. We have a limited time to live and love on earth. Being more intentional about how we spend our time is one simple way to help make each day count.

In the Details

I wait for the Lord more than watchmen wait for the morning, more than watchmen wait for the morning.

PSALM 130:6 NIV

Waiting may seem like a passive pursuit. However, you actually have a choice as to how you'll spend your time. You can waste it, worry over it, or worship through it. It doesn't matter what you're waiting for—an overdue flight, the results of a medical test, an answer to prayer—choosing to worship turns waiting into watching. The more often you turn your eyes toward God, the better chance you'll have of noticing how His hand is in the details.

Just as I Am

Therefore know that the LORD your God, He is God, the faithful God who keeps covenant and mercy for a thousand generations with those who love Him and keep His commandments.

DEUTERONOMY 7:9 NKJV

Dear God, I'm a far cry from perfect, but I'm confident in the knowledge that You love me just as I am. You are the One who has begun a work in me, and You will be faithful to complete what has been started. What a thrill to know that You'll make me what You want me to be.

Sense of Wonder

Far and wide they'll come to a stop,
they'll stare in awe, in wonder.
Dawn and dusk take turns calling,
"Come and worship."

PSALM 65:8 MSG

Children are known for their sense of wonder. Maybe that's because there's so much they don't know. The closer we draw to God, the more we realize how much we are like children—how much we really don't know. When you focus on God, take time to give yourself over to childlike wonder. That's worship in its purest and most spontaneous form. You don't need to know all the answers, as long as you know the One behind them all.

DAY 153

What Do You Worship?

Blessed are you who give yourselves over to GOD, turn your backs on the world's "sure thing," ignore what the world worships.

PSALM 40:4 MSG

What do you worship, really? Approval, financial security, youth, talent—even food— can be idols that seem to promise a happier, more satisfying life. But it's a promise that nothing and no one can keep except God. Having the picture-perfect summer home or snacking on the world's richest cheese-cake can make you feel good for a while. But they possess no real power—or answers to anything that truly matters. Only God is worthy of our worship and our love.

Worry to Prayer

*They will have no fear of bad news;
their hearts are steadfast,
trusting in the LORD.*

PSALM 112:7 NIV

The fear of bad news is what worry is all about. Trusting God is what makes that fear fade away. So the next time fear begins tugging at your heart, turn every worry that's weighing you down into a prayer. The more this becomes habit, the more you'll notice your perspective beginning to change. You'll start to anticipate seeing God bring something good out of any and every situation. For God, even bad news is an opportunity to work miracles.

Praising Others

*The Lord takes delight in his people;
he crowns the humble with victory.*

Psalm 149:4 niv

Like God, human beings respond to praise in a positive way. In fact, praise has proven just as effective as threats, promises, or any other incentive, and perhaps even more so. God is good, so let us praise the good things we see in those around us. Let us strive to emphasize the positive instead of the negative. There will always be times when we must speak the truth in love, but it is better received by a heart built with praise.

DAY 156

Your Heart Will Follow

I try to count your thoughts,
but they outnumber the grains
of sand on the beach. And when
I awake, I will find you nearby.

PSALM 139:18 CEV

Trying to comprehend an infinite God with a finite brain can leave you feeling small. That's okay. Compared to God, we are. But when we balance the fact that a God too big for our brains to hold cares for us with a love so deep that nothing, absolutely nothing, can come between us, we find peace, as well as perspective. Turn your thoughts toward God, and your heart can't help but follow.

What's in Our Hearts

Set a guard over my mouth, LORD;
keep watch over the door of my lips.

PSALM 141:3 NIV

The words we speak have power. They can hurt or heal, repel or attract. They also provide a fairly accurate barometer as to what's going on in our hearts. If you find words slipping out that you wish you could take back, return to the source. Ask God to reveal what's going on in your heart. With God's help, your words can become a welcome source of comfort and encouragement to those around you.

Even Before You Call

*You are my hiding place; you will
protect me from trouble and surround
me with songs of deliverance.*

PSALM 32:7 NIV

Having an alarm system installed in your
home can give you a sense of security. If
someone tries to break in, you can trust that
help is immediately on the way. God is a
twenty-four-hour security system. When you
call, He's there. But the truth is, God's there
even before you call. He won't hesitate to step
in to protect you, even if you're unaware of
the danger you're in.

Balancing Work and Rest

And He said to them, "Come aside by yourselves to a deserted place and rest a while." For there were many coming and going, and they did not even have time to eat.

MARK 6:31 NKJV

I had to chuckle as I read the verse that says, "Give not sleep to thine eyes" (Proverbs 6:4). I guess I don't have much trouble obeying that! I have more difficulty with "Come. . .apart. . .and rest a while" (Mark 6:31). I think I'm getting the picture though. Please help me learn to balance work and rest.

What Is Right

By your teachings, Lord, I am warned;
by obeying them, I am greatly rewarded.

PSALM 19:11 CEV

Doing the right thing comes with its own rewards. Whether it's the actual Ten Commandments or other teachings found in scripture, following what God says is right points the way toward loving relationships and a balanced life. Obedience comes with the added bonus of a guilt-free conscience and the knowledge that we're living a life that pleases the Father who so deeply loves us. These are rewards that won't tarnish with the passing of time.

A New Heart

Create in me a clean heart, O God,
and renew a steadfast spirit within me.

PSALM 51:10 NKJV

Laundry is an ongoing process. You wear clothes, soil them, and then wash them over and over again. But even after washing, clothes are never really new again. Don't confuse God's forgiveness with a trip to the Laundromat. When God forgives you, He doesn't just wash away your sins, He gives you a totally clean heart. There's no dull residue or faint stains of rebellion. You're renewed—not reused or recycled or "just like new." Your heart's new. Again.

The True You

*Test my thoughts and
find out what I am like.*

PSALM 26:2 CEV

Some women spend a great amount of
time trying to look beautiful on the outside,
while paying little attention to what's on
the inside. God's words and His Spirit can
help reveal the true you, from the inside out.
Ask God where your character needs some
touching up—or perhaps a total makeover.
See if your thoughts, your words, and your
actions line up with the woman you'd like to
see smiling back at you in the mirror each
morning.

Behind the Scenes

Show me someone who does a good job, and I will show you someone who is better than most and worthy of the company of kings.

PROVERBS 22:29 GNT

There are so many people who desire those high-profile positions, and there's nothing wrong with that; but I want to thank You for those people who are cheerfully willing to take the less noticeable jobs. Their humble contributions help things run more smoothly, and that's how I want to be— willing to do whatever needs to be done.

More Than Motherly Love

*Then our sons in their youth will
be like well-nurtured plants,
and our daughters will be like
pillars carved to adorn a palace.*

PSALM 144:12 NIV

Good food, a good night's sleep, a good
education, a good home that's safe and
overflowing with love. . . Good mothers try
to provide what their children need. But
children need more. Like adults, children
have spiritual needs as well as physical and
emotional ones. That's why praying for your
children every day is more than just a good
idea. It's a reminder that your children need
more than motherly love. They also need
their heavenly Father's involvement in their
lives.

Fully Committed

*I will never give up hope
or stop praising you.*

PSALM 71:14 CEV

Choosing to follow God is not a one-time
commitment. It's a choice that's made anew
each day. Who, or what, will you choose to
follow today? Culture or popular opinion?
Your emotions or desires? Or God and His
Word? Staying consistently committed to
anything—a diet, an exercise program, a
spouse, or God—takes effort. But with God,
His own Spirit strengthens us and gives us
hope to help us remain fully committed
to Him.

Trusting in Father God

*I've cultivated a quiet heart.
Like a baby content in its mother's
arms, my soul is a baby content.*

PSALM 131:2 MSG

Picture a well-fed newborn resting in her
mother's arms, peacefully gazing up into
her eyes. That's contentment. No worrying
about "Does this diaper make me look fat?"
No fears over "Will social security be around
when I retire?" No burning desire for a
nicer stroller or a bigger crib. Allow God to
baby you. Gaze into His eyes by recalling the
ways He's provided for you. Cultivate contentment by trusting Him as a mother is
trusted by her child.

It's a Relationship

In the morning, LORD, you hear my voice;
in the morning I lay my requests before
you and wait expectantly.

PSALM 5:3 NIV

Scheduling time to pray and read the Bible can feel like just another item on your to-do list. But getting to know God is not a project. It's a relationship. Best friends don't spend time together just because they feel they should. They do it because they enjoy each other's company and long to know each other better. The more consistent you are in spending time with God each day, the closer "friend" you'll feel He is to you.

Expert Advice

*The words of the godly encourage
many, but fools are destroyed
by their lack of common sense.*
PROVERBS 10:21 NLT

I am amazed at the wisdom that King
Solomon extended to his son in the Proverbs, Lord. I guess he would have had
expert knowledge concerning relationships, though, since he'd been involved in
so many. I'm glad he talks about both the
good and the bad, too. It gives me courage to
choose good companions.

The Heart of Devotion

Protect me, for I am devoted to
you. Save me, for I serve you
and trust you. You are my God.

PSALM 86:2 NLT

The heart of devotion isn't duty. It's love. The deeper your love, the deeper your devotion. What does being devoted to God look like? It's characterized by a "God first," instead of "me first," mentality. While it's true that being devoted to God means you'll spend time with Him, it also means you'll give your time to others. Your love of God will spill over onto the lives of those around you. Your devotion to God is beneficial to everyone!

Great Expectations

The eyes of all look expectantly to You, and You give them their food in due season.

PSALM 145:15 NKJV

Praying without expecting God to answer is kind of like wishing on a star. You don't believe it's going to make any difference, but you do it anyway—just in case there really is something behind all those fairy tales. When you pray, do so with great expectations. God is at work on behalf of a child He dearly loves—you. Just remember, God's answers may arrive in ways and at a time that you least expect.

Exceeding Riches

*Do not be overawed when others
grow rich, when the splendor
of their houses increases.*

PSALM 49:16 NIV

It's been said that "money talks." Sometimes it yells. Loudly. The things it buys helps draw attention to those who have it and to those who would do anything to get it. But money says absolutely nothing about who a person really is—or how rich he or she truly is. You have riches that exceed what's in your bank account. Every relationship you invest in, be it with God, family, or friends, is a treasure that increases in value over time.

Following the Rules

I run in the path of your commands, for you have broadened my understanding.

PSALM 119:32 NIV

Suppose there were no traffic laws. Going out for a drive would be a dangerous endeavor. Drivers would have to fight their way down the road. Traffic would be a snarled mess. Following rules can sound like the opposite of freedom. But without rules, community turns into chaos. Following God's commands protects us from harm and helps us love God and others well. It frees us to travel the road of life unencumbered by fear, uncertainty, or insecurity.

Smoothing the Rough Edges

*How wonderful, how beautiful,
when brothers and sisters get along!*

PSALM 133:1 MSG

The feel of sandpaper rubbing against unfinished wood isn't pleasant. Neither is the experience of two good friends rubbing each other the wrong way. But when friends are authentic and vulnerable with each other, it's bound to happen—and that's a good thing. It helps bring our weaknesses to light. Helping smooth out one another's rough edges is part of God's plan. If friendship hits a rough patch, stay close and work through the friction. Let love help you grow.

Better Acquainted

*I praise you, LORD, for being my guide.
Even in the darkest night,
your teachings fill my mind.*

PSALM 16:7 CEV

Suppose you learn CPR in a first-aid class. Years later, when a child nearly drowns at a neighborhood pool, you spring into action. You know exactly what to do. The same is true with the Bible. The better acquainted you become with God's words, the more readily they come to mind when you need them most. When you're unsure of which way to turn, turn to the Bible. It will help lead you where you ultimately want to go.

He Is Near

The LORD is near to all who call on him,
to all who call on him in truth.

PSALM 145:18 NIV

Prayer is often thought to be a complex, multi-layered activity. When it comes to prayer, we wonder if we're worthy. . .if we're speaking the proper words. . .if we're in the right place. . .just to name a few of the questions we ask ourselves. To put it simply, prayer is nothing more than conversation with God—so any questions we ask ourselves should be directly related to our relationship with Him. It's often awkward to converse with someone we don't know. But once we get to know our heavenly Father, prayer will come easily.

Controlled Anger

*Don't have anything to do with
foolish and stupid arguments, because
you know they produce quarrels.
And the Lord's servant must not be
quarrelsome but must be kind to
everyone, able to teach, not resentful.*

2 TIMOTHY 2:23–24 NIV

I can't take it, Father. It sometimes seems
like others deliberately do things to upset
me. Maybe it's just how they are with everyone, but I have trouble not retaliating. I
try so hard to be like You, but it's a struggle.
Please help me control my anger; help me
not to be so sensitive.

Forgive Me, Father

Wherefore, my beloved brethren,
let every man be swift to hear,
slow to speak, slow to wrath;
For the wrath of man worketh
not the righteousness of God.

JAMES 1:19–20

I did it again, Lord. I ruined an entire evening because of something incredibly ridiculous. I didn't sleep well because I was still fuming. My anger is always such a waste of time and energy. Forgive me, Father. Give me strength to control my temper, and don't let me ruin any more evenings for myself or for others.

Games

Behold, children are a heritage from the
LORD, the fruit of the womb a reward.
PSALM 127:3 ESV

Lord, my children love it when I play with them, and sometimes my participation in their activities contributes significantly to their development. But to be honest, I'm not very good at their games. I'm often distracted by other things I need to do. Please don't let me lose sight of the truth— that playing with my children is an important accomplishment.

A Prayer for My Children

Lo, children are an heritage of the LORD:
and the fruit of the womb is his reward.

PSALM 127:3

Just the other day someone reminded me of how important it is to pray for my children. So here I am, Lord. Please protect my kids. Work in their lives, so that they will want to serve You with body, mind, and soul. Provide those things that they need, and fill them with contentment as they bask in the warmth of Your love.

A Good Influence

Be ye not unequally yoked together with unbelievers: for what fellowship hath righteousness with unrighteousness? and what communion hath light with darkness?

2 CORINTHIANS 6:14

I guess I've always wanted to give people the benefit of the doubt, but I haven't always been careful enough. I've ended up becoming too close to people who disregard You, and sometimes their influence on me has been too great. Father, please help me be friendly but not intimate with unbelievers.

God at Work

*My life is an example to many,
because you have been my
strength and protection.*

PSALM 71:7 NLT

If people follow your example, where will it lead? Will they find themselves headed toward God or away from Him? As you allow God to change you from the inside out, your life will naturally point others in His direction. Being an example worth following doesn't mean you're under pressure to be perfect. It's God's power shining through the lives of imperfect people that whispers most eloquently, "There's more going on here than meets the eye. God is at work."

God's Family

*I will give you thanks in the
great assembly; among the
throngs I will praise you.*

PSALM 35:18 NIV

There's beauty and power in drawing close
to God each morning to talk to Him about
the day ahead. But you are just one of God's
children. Sometimes it's great to get the
family together for prayer and worship. Every
Sunday, in churches around the world, that's
exactly what's happening. God's family is
getting together for a Thanksgiving celebration. Like any family get-together, your presence adds to the joy. So join in! God's church
wouldn't be the same without you.

True Lineage

*You have given me the heritage
of those who fear your name.*

Psalm 61:5 niv

Your true lineage extends far beyond the branches on your family tree. That's because you have a spiritual heritage as well as a physical one. Your family line extends back through Old and New Testament times, around the world, and right up into today. You may know some of your brothers and sisters by name. Others you may not meet until you walk the streets of heaven together. But God's children are family, linked by faith and a forever future.

A New Song

*Let the word of Christ dwell in you richly
in all wisdom; teaching and
admonishing one another in psalms and
hymns and spiritual songs, singing with
grace in your hearts to the Lord.*

COLOSSIANS 3:16

Since You came into my life, dear Jesus, I am filled with a fascinating joy. You've given me a new song, and I find myself singing it at the most unusual times. Sometimes I receive questioning looks, but it gives me an opportunity to share with others what You've done in my life. I pray they seek Your joy, too.

A Good Harvest

*And may the Lord our God show us his
approval and make our efforts successful.
Yes, make our efforts successful!*

PSALM 90:17 NLT

If you plant an apple tree, you probably
hope to enjoy its fruit someday. But hoping,
and even praying, won't guarantee a good
harvest. A fruit tree needs to be watered,
pruned, and protected from bugs, frost,
and hail. It needs God's gift of life and your
loving care. The same is true for any project
you're working on. Work hard, pray hard,
and wait patiently for God's good timing.
Then, when harvest time arrives, remember
to give thanks.

Confident Expectation

*You make my life pleasant,
and my future is bright.*

PSALM 16:6 CEV

It's been said that we don't know what the future holds, but we know who holds the future. Tomorrow is not a potluck of chance possibilities. The Bible tells us that God is at work, bringing something good out of every situation His children face. Knowing a God who deeply loves us and is in control, no matter what comes our way, allows us to hold our heads high and walk toward the future with confident expectation.

Prayer and Practice

*He renews our hopes
and heals our bodies.*

PSALM 147:3 CEV

Good health is a matter of both prayer and practice. As with every detail of our lives, God wants us to share our health concerns with Him. But God also asks us to take an active role in caring for our bodies. The way we care for a gift reveals what we truly feel about the giver, as well as what we've received. Practicing healthy habits is a thank-you note to God for His gift of life.

Preaching the Truth

Let the elders that rule well be counted worthy of double honour, especially they who labour in the word and doctrine.

1 TIMOTHY 5:17

Thank You for my pastor, dear God. He loves You; and he loves those to whom he ministers. Knowing that his desire is to present the truths of the Bible is a great comfort in a world that is full of false teachings. Bless my pastor as he continues to preach Your Word.

Bless the Pastor's Family

*We ask you, brothers, to respect
those who labor among you and are over
you in the Lord and admonish you,
and to esteem them very highly
in love because of their work.
Be at peace among yourselves.*

1 THESSALONIANS 5:12–13 ESV

I ask You, Lord, to be with my pastor's family. He puts in many long hours serving You; and although he makes a point to spend time with his wife and children, they still have to make some sacrifices. Bless each one of them as they work to bring Your love to our church and community.

Help!

*You listen to the longings of those who
suffer. You offer them hope, and you pay
attention to their cries for help.*

PSALM 10:17 CEV

Help!" is a prayer every heart knows how to
pray, even those who are unsure if there's a
God who's listening. It's a cry that acknowl-
edges that life is out of our control—and a
deep-seated hope that Someone is ultimately
in charge. Our desperate cries do not disappear into thin air. God hears every prayer,
sees every tear, and doesn't hesitate to act.
God's answers and timing are not always what
we expect, but they are what we need.

Living the Truth

*Think of the bright future waiting
for all the families of honest and
innocent and peace-loving people.*

PSALM 37:37 CEV

Honesty is more than just telling the
truth. It's living it. When you conform to the
expectations of those around you instead
of focusing on maturing into the individual
God designed you to be, you rob the world of
something priceless—the unique gift of you.
You also rob yourself of the joy and freedom
that come from fulfilling your God-given
potential. When it comes to being the true
you, honesty truly is the best policy.

Footsteps

*Don't put your life in the hands
of experts who know nothing
of life, of salvation life.*

PSALM 146:3 MSG

Those we choose to follow have power over
us. Their influence can affect our actions,
as well as our way of thinking. They can help
draw us closer or steer us farther away from
God. But sometimes we're not even aware of
whom we're letting lead. Celebrities, experts
in various fields, the media, charismatic
friends—whose footsteps are you following?
Ask God to help you discern who besides Him
is worthy to lead the way for you.

Extraordinary Treasures

Who out there has a lust for life? Can't wait each day to come upon beauty?

PSALM 34:12 MSG

God is amazingly creative and incomparably loving. Having Someone like that design a plan for your life is an exciting prospect. God promises there are good things ahead for you. That promise is enough to make each morning feel like a chest filled with treasure just waiting to be opened. Greet each new day with expectation. Invite God to join you in your search for the extraordinary treasures He's scattered throughout even the most ordinary of days.

Joyful Knowledge

*Surely goodness and mercy shall
follow me all the days of my life;
and I will dwell in the house
of the Lord forever.*

PSALM 23:6

Although the world might not think that
my circumstances always warrant a song, I
am rejoicing in the knowledge of what lies
ahead. I have perfect hope of an eternity
with You. I have joy in the belief that You are
with me each step of the way. You have put a
smile in my heart. Thank You, Lord.

Live, Love, and Grow

If I say, "My foot slips," your mercy,
O Lord, will hold me up.

PSALM 94:18 NKJV

There's safety in planting yourself in a recliner and interacting with the world via big-screen TV. No real relationships to let you down or challenge you to grow up. Nothing to risk, so no chance to fail. But nowhere in scripture do we see inaction as God's plan for our lives. We're designed to live, love, and grow. Along the way, we'll also fall. It's part of being human. God's mercy gives us the courage to risk trying again.

DAY 196

Sovereign Lord

*My eyes strain to see your rescue, to see
the truth of your promise fulfilled.*

PSALM 119:123 NLT

In an age of microwave meals, instant access, and ATMs, patience is fast becoming a lost virtue. Heaven forbid we're forced to use dial-up instead of broadband! But waiting is part of God's plan. It takes time for babies to mature, for seasons to change, for fruit to ripen, and sometimes for prayers to be answered. Having to wait on God's timing reminds us that God is not our genie in a bottle. He's our sovereign Lord.

Downright Doable

*Count yourself lucky, how happy
you must be—you get a fresh start,
your slate's wiped clean.*

PSALM 32:1 MSG

It's hard to keep moving forward if you're dragging along baggage that weighs you down. God wants to help you discard what you don't need. Insecurity, guilt, shame, bad habits, past mistakes—leave them by the side of the road. Jesus has already paid the price for their removal. Once your past is truly behind you, you'll find it much easier to persevere. Tackling only one day at a time is downright doable with God's help.

Steering Right

*In your majesty, ride out to victory,
defending truth, humility, and justice.
Go forth to perform awe-inspiring deeds!*

PSALM 45:4 NLT

Remembering that only God is God keeps us humble. Sounds simple enough. But all too often we try to grab the wheel from God's hands and steer our lives in the direction of what looks like it will make us happy instead of simply doing what God asks us to do. Invite God to expose any areas of your life where pride has you heading in the wrong direction. Ask Him to reveal to you how big He really is.

New Goals

Listen to advice and accept discipline, and at te end you will be counted amoung the wise.

PROVERBS 29:11 NIV

Sometimes I get a little discouraged, Jesus. I feel like I've reached all the goals I've set for myself and that there's nothing for me to achieve that would bring any excitement. Please give me a new outlook. Give me wisdom as I set new goals, and help me to give You the glory when I succeed.

New Challenges

*And let us consider how to stir up
one another to love and good works,
not neglecting to meet together, as is
the habit of some, but encouraging one
another, and all the more as
you see the Day drawing near.*

HEBREWS 10:24–25 ESV

Oh, how I enjoy a good challenge, Lord;
and each day challenges me anew! Thank
You for these opportunities—for each exciting adventure. My desire is that I might face
each task in a godly manner and that I might
honor You in all I say and do.

Already in Love

*I am like an olive tree growing in
God's house, and I can count on
his love forever and ever.*

PSALM 52:8 CEV

How do you love someone you can't see, hear, or touch? The same way you love an unborn child. You learn everything you can about what that child is like. You speak to it, even though it doesn't speak back. When you finally meet face-to-face, you find you're already in love. Yes, you can love someone you cannot yet see. As for God, His love for you transcends eternity. You're the child He's loved since before there was time.

DAY 202

Divine Creation

The LORD merely spoke, and the
heavens were created. He breathed
the word, and all the stars were born.

PSALM 33:6 NLT

Genesis tells us how God spoke nothing
into something. But that "something" was
not just anything. It was the divine artwork
of creation. All of creation, from the tiniest
microbe to the most expansive nebula, is
wonderful in the fullest sense of the word.
Take time to appreciate the wonder God has
woven into the world. Take a walk in a park.
Fill a vase with fresh flowers. Pet a puppy.
Plant a petunia. Then, thank God.

208

God Acts

GOD's there, listening for all who pray,
for all who pray and mean it.
PSALM 145:18 MSG

God is always attentive, listening for the voice of His children. Like a mother who hears her child's cry through a baby monitor in the middle of the night, God acts on what He hears. He draws near to comfort, protect, and guide. Never hesitate to call on Him—anytime, anywhere. He isn't bothered by your questions or put off by an overflow of emotion. What touches your life touches Him.

God's Will

But take diligent heed to do the commandment and the law, which Moses the servant of the LORD charged you, to love the LORD your God, and to walk in all his ways, and to keep his commandments, and to cleave unto him, and to serve him with all your heart and with all your soul.

JOSHUA 22:5

Lord, often in my daily planning I forget to consult You. Then I wonder why things don't work out the way I think they should. Forgive my arrogant attitude. I know that only as You guide me through the day will I find joy in accomplishments. Show me how to align my goals with Your will.

DAY 205

Godly Character

*Put on then, as God's chosen ones,
holy and beloved, compassionate hearts,
kindness, humility, meekness, and patience,
bearing with one another and, if one has
a complaint against another, forgiving
each other; as the Lord has forgiven you,
so you also must forgive. And above all
these put on love, which binds everything
together in perfect harmony.*

COLOSSIANS 3:12–14 ESV

Dear God, sometimes godly character sounds
so easy to attain when I'm sitting in church,
listening to the pastor speak. In my heart I
know I want it; in my mind I believe it's
possible. Making the ideal become reality is
much harder. I need Your strength. Please
help me develop godly character.

He Is Near!

*A hostile world! I call to GOD, I cry to
God to help me. From his palace he
hears my call; my cry brings me right
into his presence—a private audience!*

PSALM 18:6 MSG

It can be difficult to picture yourself in the
presence of Someone you cannot see. But the
Bible assures us God is near. His Spirit not
only surrounds us but also moves within us.
When God's presence feels far away, remember that what you feel is not an accurate
gauge of the truth. Read the Psalms to remind
yourself that others have felt the way you do.
Then, follow the psalmists' example.
Continue praising God and moving ahead
in faith.

Godly Patience

Put it in writing, because it is not yet time for it to come true. But the time is coming quickly, and what I show you will come true. It may seem slow in coming, but wait for it; it will certainly take place, and it will not be delayed.

HABAKKUK 2:3 GNT

I have to admit that one of the greatest challenges I face each day is the need for patience. I'm tested regularly on the subject, and too often I fail. Lord, I know I won't win this battle overnight, but with Your help, I'll daily work toward achieving godly patience.

Quiet Waters

*He makes me lie down in green
pastures, he leads me beside quiet
waters, he refreshes my soul.*

PSALM 23:2–3 NIV

God created the world in six days. Then
He took a day to sit back and enjoy all of the
good things He'd done. The Bible tells us
God doesn't tire or sleep, but even He knew
the value of a time-out. If you're weary,
or simply trying to keep up with a hectic
schedule, let God lead you beside quiet waters. Look back over what you and God have
accomplished together. Rejoice, and then
rest so God can restore.

In Prayer

*I pray that the LORD will let your
family and your descendants
always grow strong.*

PSALM 115:14 CEV

Praying for the people you care about is
one way of loving them. When you pray for
them, you invite God to work in their lives.
What more loving gift could there be than
that? But prayer also softens your own heart
toward those you're praying for. With God's
help, you feel their needs more deeply, understand their motivations more clearly, and
can forgive their faults more completely.
There's no downside to lifting those you love
up in prayer.

A Reflection of God's Character

Blessed are those who keep justice, and he who does righteousness at all times!

PSALM 106:3 NKJV

Living a moral life, a life that honors God and those around you, is righteousness in action. It's the opposite of self-righteousness. That's a life where you justify doing what you deem right, regardless of whether God agrees with your assessment. Righteousness, however, reflects God's own character. It shows you truly are His child. Your actions are not swayed by emotion, peer pressure, or personal gain. You do what's right simply because it's the right thing to do.

A Personal Relationship

*I hate all this silly religion, but you,
GOD, I trust. I'm leaping and singing
in the circle of your love.*

PSALM 31:6 MSG

Religion is man-made, not God-made.
Having a personal relationship with God is
something totally different. It's not a list of
rules and regulations or something we only
"do" on Sundays. It's a love story between
Father and child, a relationship in which
we're totally accepted and unconditionally
loved. Since we can't earn God's acceptance—
it's a free gift of grace—that means we can't
lose it either. God's acceptance releases us
from the fear of rejection, so we're free to
truly be ourselves.

Day 212

Church Decisions

Do not be anxious about anything,
but in everything by prayer and
supplication with thanksgiving let
your requests be made known to God.
And the peace of God, which surpasses
all understanding, will guard your hearts
and your minds in Christ Jesus.

Philippians 4:6–7 esv

There are many decisions being made on issues concerning our church, Father. They aren't easy decisions to make, and everyone has a different opinion on what the outcome should be. Please give us direction and unity. Work in our midst so that we might bring others into Your kingdom.

A Witness in My Community

"I know your works. Behold, I have set before you an open door, which no one is able to shut. I know that you have but little power, and yet you have kept my word and have not denied my name."

REVELATION 3:8 ESV

Lord, there are so many people in my community who either don't care about You or who think they will please You by their own merit; but several of them don't truly know You. I ask You to open doors so I may witness to them. My prayer is that many will come to You.

A Time and Place

*My dear brothers and sisters,
take note of this: Everyone should
be quick to listen, slow to speak
and slow to become angry, because
human anger does not produce the
righteousness that God desires.*

JAMES 1:19–20 NIV

One of the most interesting stories in Your Word is about the time You cleansed the temple. It has taught me that there is a time and place for anger. Sin is always something that should invoke fury. Just help me to direct my anger at the sin and not the sinner.

Teaching Children

We will not hide them from their children, shewing to the generation to come the praises of the LORD, and his strength, and his wonderful works that he hath done.

PSALM 78:4

There's so much I need to teach my children about You, Lord. Throughout their lives there will be so many questions. They will face people and situations that will cause them to doubt You. Give me opportunities to instill Your Word so that when doubts come, they'll stand strong.

He's in Control

The LORD is close to the brokenhearted and saves those who are crushed in spirit.

PSALM 34:18 NIV

Putting your faith in Jesus doesn't mean you'll never have a broken heart. Scripture tells us even Jesus wept. Jesus knew the future. He knew His heavenly Father was in control. He knew victory was certain. But He still grieved. When your heart is broken, only God has the power to make it whole again. It won't happen overnight. But when you draw close to God, you draw close to the true source of peace, joy, and healing.

For a Purpose

*I cry out to God Most High,
to God, who vindicates me.*

PSALM 57:2 NIV

A beautiful woman like yourself was created for more than decoration. You were created for a purpose. Your purpose is not a specific job God has designated for you to accomplish. It's more like a unique spot He's designed for you to fill. God is working with you, encouraging you to grow into this "sweet spot." As you learn to lean on Him, God will help you discover the true joy and significance that come from simply being "you."

Life's Challenges

Beareth all things, believeth all things, hopeth all things, endureth all things.

1 CORINTHIANS 13:7

Life's challenge—how can I describe it? I might say it is my best-laid plans peppered with interruptions, broken equipment, lack of sleep, and the necessity to complete a task in the allotted amount of time regardless of the circumstances. It sounds rough, and it often seems that way, but with Your help, Father God, I can endure!

Your Answer

GOD's plan for the world stands up,
all his designs are made to last.

PSALM 33:11 MSG

In Exodus we read how God asked Moses to lead the children of Israel out of slavery in Egypt. Moses said yes to the leading but no to the public speaking. Moses' "no" didn't prevent God's plan from taking place. God used Aaron, Moses' brother, to be His spokesperson in Moses' stead. God's purpose and plan for this world will happen. God has given you the freewill to say whether you'll take part or not. What will your answer be?

He Is Listening

*Continue praying, keeping alert,
and always thanking God.*

COLOSSIANS 4:2 NCV

Our God is more great and mighty than our feeble human minds could ever imagine. No wonder we question how to properly speak to Him. But, amazingly, we have been welcomed into God's inner court, invited to speak as we see fit, and promised that when we do, He will always be listening. This is clearly beyond our comprehension, and yet it's true. Our hearts should always be full of thanks for our heavenly Father's welcoming arms.

Extend Kindness and Hospitality

Contribute to the needs of the saints and seek to show hospitality.

ROMANS 12:13 ESV

We live in a close-knit community, Lord. In some ways it's nice because we all stick together. At the same time, it can be really hard for newcomers. Some of us try to welcome them, but they often move away before long. Help us, Father, to be more open to new residents in our town.

More Than Enough

*I have God's more-than-enough,
more joy in one ordinary day than
they get in all their shopping sprees.*

PSALM 4:7 MSG

An "abundant life" is not something we can pick up at the mall or purchase online. It comes from recognizing how much we receive from God each and every day. While some of our abundance may come in the form of possessions, the overflow of an abundant life ultimately comes from what fills our hearts, not our closets. Resting in God's "more-than-enough" can transform a desire to acquire into a prayer of thanksgiving for what we've already been given.

How Will You Praise?

*Sing to the LORD a new song,
for he has done marvelous things.*

PSALM 98:1 NIV

Consider the wide variety of ways we can tell people we love how wonderful they are: send flowers, hire a skywriter, write a poem, proclaim it via Twitter, send a card, share a hug. The list goes on and on. The same is true for the ways we can praise God. We can pray, sing, dance, write our own psalm, use our God-given talents and re-sources in ways that honor Him. What novel way will you praise God today?

The Ultimate Sacrifice

I am God Most High! The only sacrifice I want is for you to be thankful and to keep your word.

PSALM 50:14 CEV

In the Old Testament, we read about God's people offering sacrifices to pay the price for their rebellion against God. In the New Testament, these sacrifices disappear—except one. When Jesus willingly went to the cross for us, He became the ultimate sacrifice. His death paid for the wrongs we've done once and for all. Each time we choose to follow God instead of our own hearts, we offer a sacrifice of thanks in return for all Jesus has done.

Christ Understands Loneliness

*"I've called your name.
You're mine."*
ISAIAH 43:4 MSG

Lord, how alone You must have been in the garden when the disciples fell asleep. And when God turned His back as You hung on the cross—was there anything to compare to what You felt? Yet You did it willingly. You understand when I'm lonely, and I thank You for being there during those times.

DAY 226

An All-the-Time Thing!

*Pray diligently. Stay alert, with
your eyes wide open in gratitude.*
COLOSSIANS 4:2 MSG

Prayer is not a sometimes thing. It's an all-
the-time thing! We need to pray every day,
being careful to keep the lines of communi-
cation open between God and ourselves all
through the day, moment by moment. When
we make this a habit, we won't miss the
many gifts of grace that come our way. And
we won't forget to notice when God answers
our prayers.

A Great Enterprise

*Unless the LORD builds the house,
the builders labor in vain.
Unless the LORD watches over the city,
the guards stand watch in vain.*

PSALM 127:1 NIV

Working hard without God is simply hard work. Working hard with God's help can be part of a great enterprise. When you honor God with what you do—by turning to Him with your decisions, treating coworkers as people God dearly loves, and doing your job as if God were your boss—your time on the job is transformed into a time of worship. Your job title isn't as significant as your willingness to let God work through you.

An Obedient Heart

Jesus said unto him, Thou shalt love the Lord thy God with all thy heart, and with all thy soul, and with all thy mind.

MATTHEW 22:37

Sometimes I get so frustrated, Lord. I've asked what You want from me, but it seems You've remained silent. Then I realize that there are specifics in Your Word that I should automatically be doing. I haven't always been obedient to those, so how can I expect to know more? Forgive me, Father. I want to obey.

Bearable Burdens

O come, let us sing unto the LORD:
let us make a joyful noise to the rock
of our salvation. Let us come before his
presence with thanksgiving, and make
a joyful noise unto him with psalms.

PSALM 95:1–2

Lord, we sometimes sing a song about being happy because You took our burdens all away. I guess You really just make the burdens more bearable. Still, that's something great to sing about, and it does bring happiness. I'm so glad You're there to lighten the load.

Let Your Worship Flow

On your feet now—applaud GOD!
Bring a gift of laughter, sing
yourselves into his presence.

PSALM 100:1 MSG

Sunday mornings at church are often
referred to as a "worship service." But worship isn't a service or duty. It's a response.
It's your personal reply to God's goodness,
power, majesty, and love. If worship isn't
how you react when you draw near to God,
perhaps you need to draw closer. Read the
Psalms aloud. Pray with your arms out-
stretched and your face flat on the floor.
Get alone with the Creator of the universe
and let your worship flow.

Big and Little Ways

He covers the heavens with clouds,
provides rain for the earth, and makes
the grass grow in mountain pastures.

PSALM 147:8 NLT

God provides for us in so many ways that it's easy to take them for granted. The fact that the sun rises each morning, encouraging crops to grow, or that our heart takes its next beat and our lungs their next breath are just a few of the countless gifts we receive from God's almighty hand. As you go through the day, consider the big and little ways God meets your needs. Then take time at the day's end to give thanks.

From the Inside Out

*With your very own hands you formed
me; now breathe your wisdom over
me so I can understand you.*

PSALM 119:73 MSG

God isn't concerned with appearances. The
Bible tells us God looks at peoples' hearts
instead of what's on the outside. Perhaps
that's because appearances can be deceiving.
A woman can be beautiful in the world's eyes,
while her heart nurtures pride, deceit, lust,
greed, or a host of other unlovely traits.
By learning to look at people the way God
does, from the inside out, we may discover
beauty in others—and in ourselves—that
we've never noticed before.

Center of Our Lives

The apostles often met together and prayed with a single purpose in mind.

ACTS 1:14 CEV

What do you do when you get together with the people you're close to? You probably talk and laugh, share a meal, maybe go shopping together or work on a project together. But do you ever pray together?

If prayer is the center of our lives, then we will want to share this gift of grace with those with whom we're closest.

A Peek at Heaven

*"With you, Lord, is unfailing love. . . .
You reward everyone according
to what they have done."*

PSALM 62:12 NIV

Revelation, the final book of the Bible, gives us a peek at what heaven will be like. One thing we discover is that we'll be rewarded for what we've done here on earth. But instead of putting these rewards on display in our heavenly mansions, we're told that the elders in the group will lay these rewards before God's throne. That's truly where they belong. God is the one who enables and inspires us to do what's worth rewarding.

Open Your Heart

*You open your hand and satisfy
the desires of every living thing.*

Psalm 145:16 niv

Our hearts are needy. They cry out for love, relief, pleasure, and purpose. They cry out for what they see on TV. Only God can quiet their relentless cry. That's because God is what they're actually crying out for. As we open our hearts more fully to God, we'll see more clearly that our needs are being met. What's more, we'll notice that our desires are changing, aligning themselves more and more with God's own.

A Comforting Haven

This is my commandment, That ye love one another, as I have loved you.

JOHN 15:12

Lord, let my home be a comforting haven for my family and friends. May it be a place where they can momentarily escape the pressures of this world. Help me to do my best to make it a place where people will know they are loved by me and, more importantly, by You.

Eternally Trustworthy

Far better to take refuge in GOD than trust in people; far better to take refuge in GOD than trust in celebrities.

PSALM 118:8–9 MSG

Trust is a gift. If we're wise, we extend it to those who are worthy of receiving it. Witnessing character traits such as honesty, integrity, loyalty, and love in a person's life lets us know that our trust hasn't been misplaced. But even trustworthy people let us down on occasion. The same cannot be said of God. God never falters or fails. He is eternally trustworthy. What do you need to trust God for today?

Surge of Gratitude

Now I'm alert to GOD's ways;
I don't take God for granted.

PSALM 18:21 MSG

The phrase "Thank God!" has lost much of its meaning these days. People use it interchangeably with expressions such as, "Wow!" "Thank goodness!" or "I really lucked out!" That's because people feel a surge of gratitude when good things happen to them, but not all of them are certain where they should direct their thanks. You've caught a glimpse of God's goodness. You know who is behind the blessings you receive. Don't hesitate to say, "Thank God!" and mean it.

To Be Like Jesus

*He that saith he abideth in
him ought himself also so
to walk, even as he walked.*

1 JOHN 2:6

Father, I was amazed to see a very attractive, well-dressed lady go out of her way to help an individual of completely opposite description. The dirt and smell didn't seem to bother her, and the heartfelt hug so brightened the other person's countenance. I thought how like You the lady was—how like You I want to be.

The Compassionate Side

But you, Lord, are a compassionate and gracious God, slow to anger, abounding in love and faithfulness.

PSALM 86:15 NIV

Without love and compassion, an all-powerful God would be something to fear instead of Someone to trust. That's one reason why Jesus came to earth: to help us see the compassionate side of the Almighty. Throughout the Gospels, we read how Jesus reached out to the hurting—the outcasts, the infirm, the poor, and the abandoned. He didn't turn his back on sinners, but embraced them with open arms. His arms are still open. Will you run toward His embrace?

Your Character Shines

*Only you can say that I am
innocent, because only your
eyes can see the truth.*

PSALM 17:2 CEV

Not everyone will understand the unseen
story behind what you say and do. There
will be times when you're misunderstood,
slandered, or even rejected. This is when
your true character shines through. How you
respond to adversity and unfair accusations
says a lot about you and the God you serve.
Ask God to help you address any blind spots
you may have about your own character.
Treat your critics with respect. Then move
ahead with both confidence and humility.

Ability to Love

God, who is rich in mercy, for his great love wherewith he loved us, even when we were dead in sins, hath quickened us together with Christ.

EPHESIANS 2:4-5

Love—what a beautiful word! Yet many people are so cynical about it, dear Jesus. I guess that's because there is so much artificial affection in this world, but I'd like for people to see true love—Your love—in my life. Please give me the ability to love as You do.

Don't Lose Heart

You are my strength, I watch for you;
you, God, are my fortress,
my God on whom I can rely.

PSALM 59:9–10 NIV

Some people believe that if they follow God, life will be trouble free. Jesus doesn't seem to agree. In John 16:33 (NIV), Jesus says, "'In this world you will have trouble.'" But Jesus doesn't leave it at that. He continues, "'But take heart! I have overcome the world.'" Don't be surprised when struggle comes, but don't lose heart either. God will provide the strength you need when you need it to help you overcome whatever comes your way.

GPS for Life

GOD is fair and just; He corrects
the misdirected, sends them
in the right direction.

PSALM 25:8 MSG

When you're driving in an unfamiliar
city, a map is an invaluable tool. It can help
prevent you from taking wrong turns. If
you do wind up headed in the wrong direction, a map can help set you back on track.
God's Word and His Spirit are like a GPS for
your life. Staying in close contact with God
through prayer will help you navigate the
best route to take in this life, one decision at
a time.

Easy to Recognize

Be joyful in hope, patient in
affliction, faithful in prayer.

ROMANS 12:12 NIV

How do you build a relationship with a
friend? You spend time together. You talk
about everything, openly sharing your
hearts. Prayer is simply talking to your best
Friend. True, it's harder to understand
God's reply than it is to read a friend's text
or pick up her phone message. But the more
frequently you pray, the easier it is to recognize God's voice. So keep talking. God's
listening. With time, you'll learn how to
listen in return.

J-O-Y

Do nothing from selfish ambition or conceit, but in humility count others more significant than yourselves.

PHILIPPIANS 2:3 ESV

Jesus-others-you. What a simple yet profound definition of joy. And I'm beginning to see just how much this really works. I guess that's because when You are first in my life, everything else is properly prioritized. Although putting others before myself isn't always easy, it feels wonderful when I do it.

The Power of Encouragement

As soon as I pray, you answer me; you encourage me by giving me strength.

Psalm 138:3 NLT

A word of encouragement can go a long way in strengthening our hearts. Whether that word comes from a friend, a spouse, a stranger, or straight from God's own Word, encouragement has power. It lets us know we're not alone. We have a support group cheering us on as we go through life. Out of that support group, God is our biggest fan. He wants you to succeed, and His help is just a prayer away.

Loving Generosity

*An evil person borrows and never pays
back; a good person is generous
and never stops giving.*

PSALM 37:21 CEV

Love and generosity are two sides of the
same coin. Both put the needs of others before their own. Both give without expecting
anything in return. Both make our invisible
God more visible to a world in need. As our
love for those around us grows, generosity
can't help but follow suit. Today take time
to become more aware of the needs of those
around you. Then ask God to help you act on
what you see with loving generosity.

Reaching Out

For great is your love,
reaching to the heavens;
your faithfulness reaches to the skies.

PSALM 57:10 NIV

I used to love Monday holidays, Lord. The
long weekends, the picnics, and family
fun—I have great memories. But now it's
different. I live too far away to go home. My
friends are with their families, and I don't
want to intrude. But I'm lonely. Please ease
that emptiness, and help me reach out to
others in similar situations.

The Test of Time

*The LORD is trustworthy in all he
promises and faithful in all he does.*

PSALM 145:13 NIV

There's an old saying that warns, "Promises are made to be broken." With God, the opposite is true. The Bible is filled with promises God has made and kept. With a track record like that, it means you can trust God's Word and His love for you. He remains faithful, even if your faithfulness to Him wavers from time to time. God and His promises have stood the test of time and will remain steadfast throughout eternity.

Enough!

What you're after is truth from the inside out. Enter me, then; conceive a new, true life.

PSALM 51:6 MSG

God knows the truth about you—and He wants you to know it, too. He wants you to put away the lies you've been listening to, the ones that whisper, "I'm not enough— smart enough, pretty enough, young enough, successful enough, loved enough, good enough." Whatever "not enough" you struggle with, ask God to help you see the truth. Then dare to go a step further by not only accepting the truth about yourself but also living your life in light of it.

Provision for Missionaries

*But my God shall supply all your
need according to his riches
in glory by Christ Jesus.*

PHILIPPIANS 4:19

In Your Word, You've commanded us to take the gospel to all nations. You've also said that when we're obedient, You'll meet our needs. Please meet the needs of our missionaries, Lord. Provide what they need physically and spiritually, and let many souls be saved as a result.

One Day at a Time

Invigorate my soul so I can praise you well, use your decrees to put iron in my soul.

PSALM 119:175 MSG

A marathon runner doesn't start out running twenty-six miles. She has to start slow, remain consistent, and push herself a bit farther day by day. That's how endurance is built. The same is true in life. If what lies ahead seems overwhelming, don't panic thinking you need to tackle everything at once. Ask God to help you do what you can today. Then celebrate the progress you've made, rest, and repeat. Endurance only grows one day at a time.

Hallmark of Integrity

*I will lead a life of integrity
in my own home.*

PSALM 101:2 NLT

Chameleons may be interesting to watch on the nature channel, but they're not something worth emulating in terms of character. Consistency in the way we live our lives—whether we're on the job, at home with family, or out on the town with friends—is a hallmark of integrity. If how we act is dependent on who we're with, we may be seeking the approval of others more than seeking God. In terms of integrity, whose approval are you seeking today?

Under God's Protection

*Let all who take refuge in you be glad;
let them ever sing for joy. Spread your
protection over them, that those who
love your name may rejoice in you.*

PSALM 5:11 NIV

In the Old Testament, God designates cities of refuge. These were places where people who'd accidentally killed someone could flee. Here they'd be safe from the vengeance of angry relatives until they'd received a fair trial or had proven their innocence. God is a place of refuge for His children. No matter what happens, you're under God's protection. Flee to Him in prayer when you feel under attack. God provides a safe haven where truth will be brought to light.

A Friendlier World

*And he said unto them, Go ye
into all the world, and preach
the gospel to every creature.*

MARK 16:15

Dear God, I was just noticing all the people around me who really could use a friend. For whatever reason, they're alone and hurting. I need to reach out to them. I ask You to give me opportunities and ideas to let them know I care. Let me make the world a little friendlier for them.

Justice Will Prevail

For all who are mistreated,
the LORD brings justice.

PSALM 103:6 CEV

If watching the evening news leaves you feeling that life isn't fair, take it as a sign that you've inherited your heavenly Father's sense of justice. The way people are treated in this world is not always fair or loving. Sometimes they're used, abused, and then tossed aside. But with God, justice will prevail. God knows each person's story and will make things right in His perfect time and in His wise and loving ways.

Moving Mountains

*Only you are God! And your power
alone, so great and fearsome,
is worthy of praise.*

PSALM 99:3 CEV

God's power is mightier than any created thing. After all, God simply spoke, and the power of His words brought everything else into existence. That kind of power can move mountains—or change lives. God's power is at work to help you accomplish things you never would have dreamed of doing on your own. Whatever God leads you to do, He will provide the power you need to see it through.

Deeper Love

"You shall love the Lord your God with all your heart and with all your soul and with all your mind."

MATTHEW 22:37 ESV

I say I love You, Father, although I'm not sure it goes as deep as it should. I want it to though. I want to be so in love with You that it shows in every aspect of my life. Help me to develop the intimacy with You that I should have.

A Heavenly Perspective

*You will show me the way of life,
granting me the joy of your
presence and the pleasures
of living with you forever.*

PSALM 16:11 NLT

Johann Wolfgang von Goethe wrote, "Life is the childhood of our immortality." In light of eternity, you're just a kid—regardless of your age. In today's youth-obsessed society, keeping your "true" age in mind can help you see each day from a more heavenly perspective. Hold on to your sense of childlike wonder. Allow it to inspire awe, thanks, praise, and delight. Draw near to your heavenly Father and celebrate. There's so much more to your life than meets the eye.

Loving Respect

*Come, my children, listen as I
teach you to respect the LORD.*

PSALM 34:11 CEV

Consider the teachers and leaders that
have helped draw you closer to God. These
people are worthy of your thanks and
prayers, but they're also worthy of your
respect. The Bible tells us God is the power
behind those in authority. But these people
are still human. They make mistakes. They
make decisions we don't always agree with.
We aren't asked to blindly follow, but we
are asked to love. Respect is one side of that
love.

Those Left Behind

"Truly, I say to you, there is no one who has left house or wife or brothers or parents or children, for the sake of the kingdom of God, who will not receive many times more in this time, and in the age to come eternal life."

LUKE 18:29–30 ESV

Father, I'd like to take just a moment to pray for the extended families of missionaries. We often forget that as obedient servants take Your gospel abroad, their relatives are left behind. The separation can be difficult. Ease the loneliness. Bless each family member in a special way.

In His Hand

*Whoever dwells in the shelter
of the Most High will rest in
the shadow of the Almighty.*

PSALM 91:1 NIV

Picture a hammock in the shade of two leafy trees, swaying gently in the breeze. Now picture yourself nestled there, eyes closed, totally relaxed. This is what it's like to rest in the shadow of the Almighty. Knowing that God holds you tenderly in His hand, offering protection, comfort, and grace, allows you to let go of your fears and concerns. God knows about them all. Rest in the fact that scripture says nothing is impossible with God.

Opportunities to Serve

*Serve the LORD with
gladness; come before
His presence with singing.*

PSALM 100:2 NKJV

We live in a needy world. People around
the globe need food and medical care.
People in our city need shelter. Our church
needs volunteers to serve in the nursery.
We can't fill every need. And God doesn't
expect us to. We have limited time, energy,
and resources. That's why prayer is such an
important part of serving. Only with God's
help will we have the wisdom and courage to
say yes or no to the opportunities that
surround us.

One by One

*Search me, God, and know
my heart; test me and
know my anxious thoughts.*

PSALM 139:23 NIV

Women have a reputation as worriers. But that's not a reputation God wants you to reinforce. God offers peace in place of worry and anxiety. Who wouldn't want to accept a trade like that? When your anxious thoughts start steamrolling their way through your mind, treat yourself like a toddler. Put yourself in a time-out. Close your eyes, breathe deeply, and give God your worries one by one. Allow God to quiet your mind and your heart.

Modest Example

In like manner also, that women adorn
themselves in modest apparel, with
shamefacedness and sobriety; not with
braided hair, or gold, or pearls, or costly
array; but (which becometh women
professing godliness) with good works.

1 TIMOTHY 2:9–10

So many people think that modesty is only a clothing issue, but You've shown me that it's so much more. It's an attitude akin to humility, and it's what You want from me. Even in this You set the example for me, Jesus. Help me to follow the pattern You've given me.

Our Labor and God's Love

You will eat the fruit of your labor;
blessings and prosperity will be yours.
PSALM 128:2 NIV

Some blessings are ours simply because
God loves us. Other blessings come as a result of working with God. When it's within
our ability, God expects us to play an active
role in answering our own prayers. We pray
for provision yet continue to perform faithfully at work. We pray for better marriages
yet do our part to love and forgive. We pray
for better health yet watch what we eat.
Between our labor and God's love, we're
doubly blessed.

DAY 268

Rest in God

*You've kept track of my every toss
and turn through the sleepless nights,
each tear entered in your ledger,
each ache written in your book.*

PSALM 56:8 MSG

Insomnia can feel like a curse. Your mind races and your body aches for rest. When sleep is elusive, rest in God. Set your mind on Him, instead of on what lies heavy on your heart. Meditate on a single verse of scripture, allowing the truth of God's words to release the tension from your body and the muddle in your mind. Curl up in the crook of God's arm, and let Him draw you toward dreams worth dreaming.

Worthy of Awe

Make vows to the LORD your God,
and keep them. Let everyone bring
tribute to the Awesome One.

PSALM 76:11 NLT

People use the word awesome to describe everything from landing a difficult snowboarding maneuver to evaluating a pair of Jimmy Choo shoes. But at the heart of the word lies its original intent: declaring something worthy of our awe. When it comes to inspiring awe, nothing can compare to God. Everything He does and everything He is, is totally awesome. Really. Allow the truth of what you know about God to really sink in. Wonder—and awe—is certain to follow.

On Behalf of Our Soldiers

Have not I commanded thee?
Be strong and of a good courage;
be not afraid, neither be thou
dismayed: for the LORD thy God is
with thee whithersoever thou goest.

JOSHUA 1:9

There is a very special group of Americans whom I'd like to bring before You, Father. They are our servicemen and -women. So many of them are in harm's way, Lord. They need Your protection in a way I cannot even comprehend. Please put a hedge around them. Bring them safely home.

What You Know

Without wisdom, knowledge is just a
bunch of information. Who cares if you
have all the answers but are clueless when
it comes to applying what you know? If you
want to be a wise woman, the Bible says all
you need to do is ask. God will impart to you
understanding and insight that goes beyond
your own personal experience. Once you
understand the wise thing to do, all that
remains is doing it.

A Measure of Success

They are like trees growing beside a stream, trees that produce fruit in season and always have leaves. Those people succeed in everything they do.

PSALM 1:3 CEV

How do you measure success? By your title? Your weight? Your net worth? The opinion of others? God's measure of success has little to do with accolades, appearance, acquisitions, or admiration. According to the Bible, the key to real success is love. The more we love God and others, the more successful we are at fulfilling what God has planned for our lives. Want to be a truly successful woman? Serve others with a humble heart.

A Modest Heart

But let it be the hidden man of the heart, in that which is not corruptible, even the ornament of a meek and quiet spirit, which is in the sight of God of great price.

1 PETER 3:4

I guess we all like to receive praise from time to time, and in moderation it's probably good for us. But, Father, give me a modest heart about the honor when it does come. Don't let me become puffed with pride. I want to give the glory to You, for without You I am nothing.

A Fresh Page

*I feel put back together, and I'm
watching my step. GOD rewrote
the text of my life when I opened
the book of my heart to his eyes.*

PSALM 18:24 MSG

God can rewrite your life's story line. It's
true that what's done is done—God won't
change the past—but He can change how you
see it. He can reveal how He has woven
themes of redemption and blessing
throughout what once looked hopeless. He
can also change how the past affects you.
Through His power, God can free you from
the bondage of bad habits and past mistakes. As for the future, that's a fresh page.

What will God and you co-write?

Your Spiritual Journey

*Blessed are those whose strength is in
you, whose hearts are set on pilgrimage.*

PSALM 84:5 NIV

You're embarking on a lifelong spiritual
journey. It's a pilgrimage that will follow a
different path than that of anyone else who
has ever desired to grow closer to God. The
prayers you pray, how quickly you mature,
the battles you fight, the challenges you
overcome, and the person you become will
all add up to a one-of-a-kind adventure.
Look to God instead of comparing yourself
to others to gauge how far you've come and
what direction you're headed next.

Every Twist and Turn

I trust in you, LORD; I say, "You are my God." My times are in your hands.

PSALM 31:14–15 NIV

Change can be exciting. It can also be uncomfortable, unwanted, and at times even terrifying. If you're facing change and find yourself feeling anxious or confused, turn to the God of order and peace. He holds every twist and turn of your life in His hands. Try looking at change through God's eyes, as an opportunity for growth and an invitation to trust Him with your deepest hopes and fears.

Peaceful Rest

Take my yoke upon you, and learn of me; for I am meek and lowly in heart: and ye shall find rest unto your souls.

MATTHEW 11:29

How beautiful to watch a sleeping child! With an arm wrapped gently around his teddy bear and his thumb in his mouth, he embodies peacefulness. As I watch him, I am reminded that You've promised peaceful rest to those in Your care. Oh, how I thank You for this!

A Prayer Away

Praise be to the Lord, to God our Savior, who daily bears our burdens.

PSALM 68:19 NIV

Some things are too heavy to carry alone. A couch, for instance. Or a washing machine. The same is true for the mental and emotional burdens we bear. The good news is that strength, peace, comfort, hope, and a host of other helping hands are only a prayer away. We're never alone in our pain or struggle. God is always near, right beside us, ready to help carry what's weighing us down.

Incomparable God

The LORD is my strength and my shield;
my heart trusts in him, and he helps me.
PSALM 28:7 NIV

A rock, a fortress, a warrior, a king—the
Bible uses many metaphors to describe
God. Since no single word can wholly
describe our infinite, incomparable God,
word pictures help us better connect a God
we cannot see with images that we can. If
your attitude could use a boost of strength
and confidence, picture God as your shield.
He is always there to protect you, to shelter
you, and to guard your heart and mind.

New Every Morning

It is of the LORD's mercies that we are not consumed, because his compassions fail not. They are new every morning: great is thy faithfulness.

LAMENTATIONS 3:22–23

I really didn't want to get up this morning, Father. My blankets seemed like good protection from the cares of the day. But when I saw the glorious sunrise and heard the cheerful, singing birds, I was reminded that Your compassions are new every morning. I knew everything would be fine. Thank You for Your faithfulness.

The Ups and Downs

*GOD will help me. At dusk, dawn,
and noon I sigh deep sighs—he hears,
he rescues. My life is well and whole,
secure in the middle of danger.*

PSALM 55:16–17 MSG

You may think you're living a balanced life.
You eat right, exercise regularly, and try to
limit stress by allowing breathing room in
your schedule. But if you're not taking care
of your spiritual needs, your life is still out
of balance. It's like trying to take a solo see-
saw ride. It can't be done. Welcoming God
into the ups and downs of each day is the key
to wholeness. Is God's peace the missing
piece in your life?

Alone Time with God

But Jesus often withdrew
to the wilderness for prayer.

LUKE 5:16 NLT

God is always with us, even when we're too busy to do more than whisper a prayer in the shower or as we drive the car. But if even Jesus needed to make time to get away by Himself for some alone-time with God, then we certainly need to do so, too. In those quiet moments of prayer, by ourselves with God, we will find the grace we need to face our busy lives.

Bless You

*May God be gracious to us and bless us
and make his face shine on us.*

PSALM 67:1 NIV

When people speak of "blessings," they're often referring to words. Blessings are given at meals and weddings. "Bless you" is even said after a sneeze. The words we say can be as much of a gift as the blessings we can hold in our hands. What would God have you say to the people you meet today? Consider how you can bless others with your words—then speak up. A good word can often be the perfect gift.

Healing Our Hurts

And we know that God causes all things to work together for good to those who love God, to those who are called according to His purpose.

ROMANS 8:28 NASB

I was just trying to help. I knew from personal experience that he was about to make a mistake. I tried to be gentle and loving, but he became so angry, telling me it was none of my business. Now he won't even speak to me, and that hurts. Please heal the breach, Father.

Cleansing Rains

*And be renewed in
the spirit of your mind.*

EPHESIANS 4:23

That refreshing rain! Oh, how badly we needed it. The fields were parched and the rivers drying. Just when we thought we could take no more of the heat, You sent the cool, cleansing rains. Now the garden's growing, the streams are flowing, and our hearts are offering thanks!

Light in the Darkness

*Then spake Jesus again unto them, saying,
I am the light of the world: he that
followeth me shall not walk in darkness,
but shall have the light of life.*

JOHN 8:12

I've noticed many disturbing events in my community, Lord—activities that in no way glorify You. I don't become involved, but some Christians do, either out of peer pressure or simply because they don't know it's wrong. Open their eyes. Help us band together to offer Your light in the darkness.

Christian Community

"You are the light of the world. A city set on a hill cannot be hidden. Nor do people light a lamp and put it under a basket, but on a stand, and it gives light to all in the house. In the same way, let your light shine before others, so that they may see your good works and give glory to your Father who is in heaven."

MATTHEW 5:14–16 ESV

I'm thankful for the Christians in my town, dear God. It is such a blessing to fellowship with them. Recently we've started a Bible study that is mostly intended to be an outreach program. Please let it be successful for Your kingdom.

The Center of God's Will

I know that there is nothing better for people than to be happy and do good while they live. That each of them may eat and drink, and find satisfaction in all their toil—this is the gift of God.

ECCLESIASTES 3:12–13 NIV

It's a fast-paced world where everyone wants to get ahead, Father. Sometimes contentment is frowned upon. Some folks think of it as laziness or lack of motivation. But I know that if I am in the center of Your will, I'll be content. That's the only true contentment there is.

The Right Path

Show me the right path, O LORD;
point out the road for me to follow.

PSALM 25:4 NLT

I'm a little concerned about the effect some
of my neighbors might be having upon my
children, Lord. I've tried to bring them up
according to Your Word, but peer pressure
can be quite strong. Please help them to be
faithful and to stay on the right path.

Satisfied

*But godliness with
contentment is great gain.*

I TIMOTHY 6:6

It doesn't take much to please a kitten, does
it, Lord? Put him on your lap, rub his head,
and listen to him purr. What contentment! I
wish I were like that, but it seems the more I
gain, the more I strive for. There's not much
contentment in that. Let me learn from the
cat to be satisfied no matter what!

Abundant Life

*Take heed, and beware of
covetousness: for a man's life
consisteth not in the abundance
of the things which he possesseth.*

LUKE 12:15

Sometimes my attitude is so "poor me" that
I even get sick, Father. I keep thinking that
if only I could have this or that, life would
be easier. I know I'm missing out on a truly
abundant life by whining so much, and I ask
You to forgive me. Fill me with contentment.

Rewarding Work

*Give her of the fruit of her hands;
and let her own works praise
her in the gates.*

PROVERBS 31:31

I am exhausted, Lord, but I don't think
I've ever felt better! There's nothing quite
like a hard day's work to bring a tremen-
dous amount of satisfaction. And I'm really
anticipating the good night's sleep ahead
because I know I pleased You with my effort
today.

Nothing too Insignificant

*Oh that men would praise the Lord
for his goodness, and for his wonderful
works to the children of men!*

PSALM 107:8

I am convinced, Father, that one reason You
bring children across our paths is to teach
us important lessons. It wasn't long ago that
I heard a small child thanking You for many
things. "And thank You for the lightning
bugs," he said. What a simple reminder that
there's nothing too insignificant for which to
offer thanks.

For Good

And we know that all things work together for good to them that love God, to them who are the called according to his purpose.

ROMANS 8:28

I feel like crying, Father. We planned to leave for vacation next week, but today my husband was a victim of downsizing. Vacation is now out of the question. He has to find a new job, or we won't be able to pay our bills. Help me to remember that all things work together for good to those who love You.

Through the Storms

*God is our refuge and strength,
a very present help in trouble.*

PSALM 46:1

I was staying on top of my duties for once, Lord. But then the dryer quit working, and I still had piles of laundry to finish. It was fun hanging the clothes out to dry and pretending I was a pioneer—until the rains came. The clothes were drenched, and so were my spirits. I wanted to give up. Please remind me that You are with me through the storms.

Family Blessings

And if it seem evil unto you to serve the LORD, choose you this day whom ye will serve; whether the gods which your fathers served that were on the other side of the flood, or the gods of the Amorites, in whose land ye dwell: but as for me and my house, we will serve the LORD.

JOSHUA 24:15

Among Your many blessings, my family ranks near the top. They share my joys and help bear my burdens. Dear Jesus, I know that You selected each of my relatives to be a part of my life in a special way, and I thank You for each of them. May I bring happiness to them in some way, too!

To God Be the Glory!

But the Lord stood with me and strengthened me, so that the message might be preached fully through me, and that all the Gentiles might hear. Also I was delivered out of the mouth of the lion. And the Lord will deliver me from every evil work and preserve me for His heavenly kingdom. To Him be glory forever and ever. Amen!

2 Timothy 4:17–18 nkjv

Lord, when I think about the world in which I'm raising my children, I tremble. Crime, hatred, terrorism—they're everywhere, and they scare me. I know I should remember that You are in control, and I try, but sometimes I get too caught up in what's happening. Please forgive me, and give me peace.

He's Waiting. . .

The eyes of the Lord watch over
those who do right, and his
ears are open to their prayers.

1 PETER 3:12 NLT

You don't have to try to get God's attention.
He is watching you right now. His ear is tuned
to your voice. All you need to do is speak, and
He will hear you. Receive the gift of grace He
gives to you through prayer. Tell God your
thoughts, your feelings, your hopes, your
joys. He's waiting to listen to you.

Reminders of Great Blessing

Every good gift and every perfect gift is from above, and cometh down from the Father of lights, with whom is no variableness, neither shadow of turning.

JAMES 1:17

We had a family reunion the other day, and I was surprised at how much our family has grown. I used to never really enjoy these gatherings, but this time was different. It was a reminder of the great blessing You've bestowed on me. I realized, also, the opportunity I had to present a testimony of Your love to those who'd never heard. I guess reunions aren't so bad after all.

Courageous for God

*Be strong and of good courage, fear not,
nor be afraid of them: for the Lord thy
God, he it is that doth go with thee;
he will not fail thee, nor forsake thee.*

DEUTERONOMY 31:6

One of the cutest songs I know is about
a child peering into a box of crayons and
comparing the colors to the Christian life.
Yellow represents the cowardly believer—
one who is afraid to share Christ's love with
others. Please don't let me be yellow. Let me
be courageous for You!

Purify Me

*Blessed are the pure in heart:
for they shall see God.*

MATTHEW 5:8

Father, please show me if the life I live is
truly pure in Your sight. In my pride, I'm
afraid I raise myself to greater heights than I
ought to where cleanliness is involved. But I
want to see myself through Your eyes. I want
to measure up to Your standards. Please
purify my attitude, Lord.

Financial Responsibilities

*But seek ye first the kingdom of God,
and his righteousness; and all these
things shall be added unto you.*

MATTHEW 6:33

It's funny, Lord. It seems like I always wish I had more money, but dealing with it can sometimes be a pain. Keeping it organized, making sure my bills are paid—at times it's overwhelming. Please give me a clear mind and wisdom to handle my financial responsibilities according to Your will.

Practicing Forgiveness

*And be ye kind one to another,
tenderhearted, forgiving one
another, even as God for
Christ's sake hath forgiven you.*

Ephesians 4:32

Growing up with ornery siblings, I had plenty of chances to practice forgiveness. I guess that's good because I still have opportunities to forgive. Sometimes it isn't easy, but it feels so much better to let go of the hurt than to hold a grudge. Thank You for giving me these occasions.

Best in Relationships

*And let us consider one another to
provoke unto love and to good works:
Not forsaking the assembling of ourselves
together, as the manner of some is;
but exhorting one another: and so much
the more, as ye see the day approaching.*

HEBREWS 10:24–25

I know that You've brought people into my
life for many different reasons, but I have to
admit that sometimes I'd like to take my dog
and move to my own island. It's hard to please
people, and it's easy to upset them. Neither
situation is pleasant for me. Lord, please help
me do my best in each relationship.

Trust and Love More

*Yet in all these things we are more than
conquerors through Him who loved us.
For I am persuaded that neither death
nor life, nor angels nor principalities nor
powers, nor things present nor things to
come, nor height nor depth, nor any
other created thing, shall be able to
separate us from the love of God.*

ROMANS 8:37–39 NKJV

I've been concentrating so much on my
grief, Lord, that I'm afraid my perspective of
You has become warped. I wonder why You
allow bad things to happen, and sometimes
I even question whether or not You really
love me. I know the truth is that You are right
there with me, wanting me to trust and love
You more. Help me keep that in focus.

Happy Times

The LORD has done it this very day;
let us rejoice today and be glad.

PSALM 118:24 NIV

A lot of times I've heard people say that
Christians can be joyful without being
happy, and I know that's true. Still, I relish
those happy times in life. It feels good to
laugh so hard that I'm crying and to smile
because I see something cute. Thank You for
giving me happy times to enjoy, dear Jesus.

The Blessing of Freedom

*Now the Lord is the Spirit; and where
the Spirit of the Lord is, there is liberty.*

2 CORINTHIANS 3:17 NKJV

It brings tears to my eyes just to hear "The
Star-Spangled Banner," and I get choked
up when I see veterans being honored. I
know it's because of the sacrifices made by
others that I have freedom to worship You
as I choose. Thank You for my country. May
I never take these liberties for granted.

Amazing Riches

Yours, O LORD, is the greatness and the power and the glory and the victory and the majesty, for all that is in the heavens and in the earth is yours. Yours is the kingdom, O LORD, and you are exalted as head above all.

1 CHRONICLES 29:11 ESV

Sometimes I find myself worrying about my financial situation. I have a tendency to forget that my Father owns the cattle on a thousand hills—and everything else, too. I know You'll take care of me. Although I might not fully understand wealth in this life, I have amazing riches to anticipate. What a thrill that is!

All Alone

But when you pray, go away by yourself, shut the door behind you, and pray to your Father in private. Then your Father, who sees everything, will reward you.

MATTHEW 6:6 NLT

Prayer takes many shapes and forms. There's the corporate kind of prayer, where we lift our hearts to God as a part of a congregation. There's also the prayer that's said quickly and on the run; the whispered cry for help or song of praise. But we need to make time in our lives for the prayer that comes out of solitude, when, in the privacy of some quiet place, we meet God's grace all alone.

God's Child

Study to shew thyself approved unto God,
a workman that needeth not to be
ashamed, rightly dividing the word of truth.

2 TIMOTHY 2:15

Do You feel welcome in my home, Father? Are You happy to be here, or are You ashamed to call me Your child? I want You to be more important in our daily lives than anything else, and I want to open our home to You to use in any way You choose.

Singing of His Love

I will sing of the LORD's great love
forever; with my mouth I will make your
faithfulness known through all generations.
I will declare that your love stands firm
forever, that you have established your
faithfulness in heaven itself.

PSALM 89:1–2 NIV

When you're filled with the love of the Lord, it's hard to contain the song that rises up in your heart. Why stop it? Let it flow! Praise makes even the hardest situation manageable. And what a great witness! When others hear you humming, when they see your passion for praise, they will wonder what you have that they don't. Join in the greatest love song of all time today— praise to the King of kings!

A Servant

Look upon me with love;
teach me your decrees.
PSALM 119:135 NLT

We're by nature very proud, Jesus. Humility certainly doesn't come easily. But You are humble, and You are the example I am to follow regardless of what comes readily. Teach me to be more like You. Teach me to be a servant.

Songs of Joy

*Whom having not seen, ye love;
in whom, though now ye see him not,
yet believing, ye rejoice with joy
unspeakable and full of glory.*

I PETER 1:8

I love listening to children singing songs about joy. They're such positive tunes, and I find myself wanting to join in. And why shouldn't I? I'm sure it would please You to hear adults belting out these joyful Sunday school verses with as much conviction as the little ones. After all, You've given us our joy.

Salvation of Loved Ones

God so loved the world, that he gave his only begotten Son, that whosoever believeth in him should not perish, but have everlasting life.

JOHN 3:16

There are many people in my family who have not accepted Your gift of salvation, dear Jesus. My most heartfelt prayer for each of them is that they will trust You. Draw each of them into Your embrace. I pray that each would receive You as Savior.

One Nation under God

*For the kingdom is the LORD's: and he is
the governor among the nations.*
PSALM 22:28

Dear God, I am so weary of the bickering
in our nation. It disturbs me to see people
attempting to remove You from schools,
courtrooms, and anywhere else they think
of. They distort history and deny that this
nation was founded with You as her leader.
Heal us, Lord. Help us return to You!

Uplifting Spirits

"Don't be afraid," he said, "for you are very precious to God. Peace! Be encouraged! Be strong!"

DANIEL 10:19 NLT

I remember when I was little how embarrassing it was to be teased about my nerdy assortment of clothing. And it hurt when the "big kids" picked on me, but You also brought people into my life who uplifted and encouraged me. What a blessing they were! Lord, let me build another person's self-esteem.

Beautiful Feet

*After that he poureth water into
a bason, and began to wash the
disciples' feet, and to wipe them with
the towel wherewith he was girded.*

JOHN 13:5

Jesus, I read the story about how You washed Your disciples' feet, and I thought about how unpleasant that might have been. Were You thinking that those same feet would carry Your gospel to the world? They were no longer appalling, but beautiful. I will wash feet if You call me to, or I'll carry Your message.

Book of Wisdom

*Incline thine ear unto wisdom, and
apply thine heart to understanding.*

PROVERBS 2:2

There are so many "how-to" books avail-
able today, Lord, and they all promise to
increase my knowledge in some area. But
not one of them gives any hope for added
wisdom. Only Your Word offers that. Thank
You for providing the means to know You
more fully and to live life more abundantly.

Emotional Struggles

He that is slow to wrath is of great understanding: but he that is hasty of spirit exalteth folly.

PROVERBS 14:29

Father, You know the emotional roller coaster I've been riding. I want to be happy for my friends when they rejoice, but the pain in my heart is so raw. It seems like my loved ones are flaunting their joy, and I can't help but react angrily. I know this hurts them and isn't pleasing to You. Please help me through this struggle.

Give Me Patience, Lord

*But let patience have her perfect work,
that ye may be perfect and entire,
wanting nothing.*

JAMES 1:4

Deadlines, sports schedules, unexpected overnight company—I'm about to pull out my hair! I know we all have our share of stress, but didn't I get an extra load this week, Father? I'm not sure what the purpose of it is, but I know there's a reason. Lord, give me patience through the ordeal, and let me please You.

In God's Eyes. . .

*He who tills his land will have plenty of food, but he who follows empty pursuits will have poverty in plenty.
A faithful man will abound with blessings, but he who makes haste to be rich will not go unpunished.*

PROVERBS 28:19–20 NASB

You know, when I was little, I had chores to do. I didn't want to do them because they didn't seem important. I wanted to do meaningful work. Now I find myself with the same attitude at times. You show me a job that needs to be done, but I ignore it because I want something more challenging. Forgive me, Lord. In Your eyes it's all important.

Prioritizing

Look carefully then how you walk, not as unwise but as wise, making the best use of the time, because the days are evil.

 EPHESIANS 5:15–16 ESV

Father, I really have a lot to do, and I'm not very good at multitasking. I need Your help each day as I organize the chores that need to be done. Show me how to prioritize my workload so that I can get things done in the most efficient manner, and let my work be pleasing in Your sight.

Don't Quit

*Though he fall, he shall not be
utterly cast down; for the Lord
upholds him with His hand.*

Psalm 37:24 nkjv

Lord, I don't want to be a quitter; but I've
tried so hard to be like You, and I keep
messing up. I know You said that with You
all things are possible, and I need to be
reminded of that daily. Don't let me give
up. Help me to remember that You aren't
finished with me yet.

Applying Wisdom

See then that you walk circumspectly,
not as fools but as wise.

EPHESIANS 5:15 NKJV

Lord, You've given me a wealth of wisdom right there in Your Word, but knowing what's there and acting upon it are two entirely different things. Sometimes my behavior is still so foolish. Forgive me, Lord. Help me not to ignore the direction You've given me. Help me to walk wisely.

In Line with the Truth

*Everything you ask for in prayer will be
yours, if you only have faith.*

MARK 11:24 CEV

Faith keeps our prayers in line with the
truth behind what we say we believe. If we
believe God loves us, believe Jesus is who He
said He was, believe God has a plan for our
lives, believe He's good, wise, and just—our
prayers will reflect these beliefs. They'll
be in line with God's will—with what God
desires for our life. These are the kind of
prayers God assures us He'll answer, in His
time and His way.

Count It All Joy

My brethren, count it all joy when you fall into various trials, knowing that the testing of your faith produces patience.

JAMES 1:2–3 NKJV

It's hard to see discouragement as a blessing, Lord. But You said we should count it as a joy. The trials will increase my patience and mold me into a more mature believer. When I look at it that way, it's much easier to thank You for the difficult times.

Godly Parents

*Train up a child in the way he
should go; and when he is old
he will not depart from it.*

PROVERBS 22:6 NKJV

Dear Lord, I got my first glimpse of You
through the lives of my parents. What a
blessing to have two such godly people as
an intimate part of my childhood and early
adult years. Thank You that they cared
enough to instill godly principles in me and
loved me enough to introduce me to You.

Fear of the Unknown

*"Can all your worries add a
single moment to your life?"*

MATTHEW 6:27 NLT

I have to laugh when I consider the silly
childhood fears I had—mostly fears of the
unknown. But when I consider the truth,
even now my fears are mostly still of the unknown. It's not so silly now, though, because
I should be trusting You instead of worrying.
Please help my thoughts to be on You.

The Widow's Mites

*And He looked up and saw the rich
putting their gifts into the treasury,
and He saw also a certain poor widow
putting in two mites. So He said, "Truly
I say to you that this poor widow has
put in more than all; for all these out of
their abundance have put in offerings
for God, but she out of her poverty put
in all the livelihood that she had."*

LUKE 21:1–4 NKJV

Lately there have been times when it's
been a little hard to tithe. We have trouble
paying our bills, so we do without things.
The worst thing, though, is thinking about
how little our meager contribution actually
benefits. Lord, I've been trying to remember the widow's mites, and that does help.
Let me take courage from her example.

Grant Me Strength

"Therefore do not worry about tomorrow, for tomorrow will worry about its own things. Sufficient for the day is its own trouble."

MATTHEW 6:34 NKJV

It's the end of another day, Father. I didn't accomplish enough, and tomorrow looms nearby with all of its expectations. I want to rejoice in the days You give me, but honestly it's been a chore merely to put one foot in front of the other. The stress of the load weighs me down. Please grant me the strength to take one step at a time.

Christ Understands

*The LORD is my strength and my
shield; my heart trusts in him.*

PSALM 28:7 NIV

Lord, You've been through things that I
will never experience, so You understand
how hard it is to forgive. Even though You've
experienced the worst insult, You never put
me down for thinking that the wrong done
to me is unbearable. Instead, You just give
me strength to do what is necessary. How
can I thank You?

Joshua's Example

And we have such trust through Christ toward God. Not that we are sufficient of ourselves to think of anything as being from ourselves, but our sufficiency is from God.

2 CORINTHIANS 3:4–5 NKJV

Joshua faced a tough challenge, didn't he, Lord? He had to get a rather difficult group of people across a huge river right at flood stage, and that was merely the beginning. But he didn't flinch. He trusted Your promises to be with him, and I can, too. Thank You for reminding me of Joshua's example right when I needed it most.

"I Love You"

Love suffers long and is kind; love does
not envy; love does not parade itself,
is not puffed up; does not behave rudely,
does not seek its own, is not provoked,
thinks no evil; does not rejoice in
iniquity, but rejoices in the truth;
bears all things, believes all things,
hopes all things, endures all things.

1 CORINTHIANS 13:4–7 NKJV

Today my little girl turned her cherubic face toward me and said so sincerely, "I love you." She doesn't fully understand, but she means it as best as she knows how. Just to hear those precious words in her sweet little voice brightened my day, and I thank You for that blessing.

Stand for Truth

"'You will not need to fight in this battle. Position yourselves, stand still and see the salvation of the LORD, who is with you, O Judah and Jerusalem!' Do not fear or be dismayed; tomorrow go out against them, for the LORD is with you."

2 CHRONICLES 20:17 NKJV

Lord, as large as my family is, there are bound to be some members whose life views are significantly different than mine. At times this gets annoying, particularly when they attempt to force their outlook on me. Give me the strength to stand for what I know to be true, and help me to love my family despite our differences.

Soothing Peace

The LORD gives his people strength.
The LORD blesses them with peace.
PSALM 29:11 NLT

Thank You, Lord, for this opportunity to bask in the peace that You offer. As I sit here in the woods, listening to the creek gently bubbling over the stones, I am reminded how Your presence in my life soothes even in the midst of chaos. I'm glad I have Your peace!

Healthy Fear

The fear of the LORD is the beginning
of wisdom; a good understanding have
all those who do His commandments.
His praise endures forever.

PSALM 111:10 NKJV

The fear of the LORD is the beginning of
wisdom" (Psalm 111:10). Sometimes this
passage from Your Word seems almost con-
tradictory, Lord. But there is healthy fear,
and then there's crippling fear. I know this
passage means that my respect of You is so
deep that I abhor sin. Please help me to have
this wise fear.

A Friend's Forgiveness

*Forbearing one another, and forgiving
one another, if any man have a quarrel
against any: even as Christ forgave
you, so also do ye.*

COLOSSIANS 3:13

I can't believe it, Father. I really messed up
this time, and my friend still forgave me. I
didn't really expect her to ever want to speak
to me again, but she hugged me and told me
we'd just start again. That felt so wonderful!
Thank You for friends who forgive.

No Excuses

*Therefore all things whatsoever
ye would that men should do to you,
do ye even so to them: for this
is the law and the prophets.*

MATTHEW 7:12

I want to say, "You don't know what that person's like. He's impossible to love!" But You told me to love my enemies. You showed me how to do this by dying for me even when my life was loathsome from sin. I was hideous, unlovable, but You still cared. I have no excuse not to love my enemies.

World Missions and Me

*And he said unto them, Go ye
into all the world, and preach
the gospel to every creature.*

MARK 16:15

Father, I believe the mission field You have
for me is right here at home, but I know You
want me to be involved in world missions
as well. Help me to faithfully pray for our
missionaries. Give me wisdom as to how You
would have me financially support them,
and show me any other way I can help them.

From Now On. . .

*Cast your burden on the LORD, and
He shall sustain you; He shall never
permit the righteous to be moved.*

PSALM 55:22 NKJV

Forgive me, Father. Time and again I've
been so stressed that I wanted to give up
on life. I tried so hard to get through each
day, but I never bothered to give my worries
to You. I've fought through each task and
brought grief to others by trying to struggle
alone, but from now on, I'm casting my
cares on You!

My Heavenly Mansion

*A tranquil heart gives life to the flesh,
but envy makes the bones rot.*

PROVERBS 14:30 ESV

Enormous homes seem to be what are
expected in this "get more" society. Calling someone's home "modest" is almost
derogatory, and that's a shame. Help me
not to envy those who have more. My home
meets my needs and gives me something to
look forward to as I anticipate my heavenly
mansion.

Open Their Hearts, Lord

Walk in wisdom toward those who are outside, redeeming the time. Let your speech always be with grace, seasoned with salt, that you may know how you ought to answer each one.

COLOSSIANS 4:5–6 NKJV

Lord, my neighbors are some of the most rude and inconsiderate people I've ever known. It's hard not to complain about them, but I don't have a right to. They aren't Christians, and I've never witnessed to them. Why would they act differently? Forgive me, Father. I will take them Your Word. Please open their hearts.

Righteous Leaders

"The God of Israel said, The Rock of Israel spoke to me: 'He who rules over men must be just, ruling in the fear of God. And he shall be like the light of the morning when the sun rises.'"

2 SAMUEL 23:3–4 NKJV

You've said that righteous leaders result in rejoicing among the people, and You've given us the opportunity to choose our leaders. With this privilege, You've given us the responsibility of electing godly people. Father, give us wisdom to recognize these individuals and to put them into office.

The Gift of Peace

*Thou wilt keep him in perfect peace,
whose mind is stayed on thee:
because he trusteth in thee.*

ISAIAH 26:3

Father, as I look around, I see so much turmoil. My heart breaks as I watch the trials people attempt to face without You in their lives. They don't realize the perfect peace that You want to give them, and many of them don't want to hear about it. Speak to their hearts. Help them accept Your gift.

Love and Fear

"And now, Israel, what does the LORD your
God require of you, but to fear the LORD
your God, to walk in all His ways and to
love Him, to serve the LORD your God with
all your heart and with all your soul."

DEUTERONOMY 10:12 NKJV

Looking at it from a human perspective, it
doesn't seem like love and fear are remotely
connected. Yet we are admonished many
times to love and fear You. It's a little hard
to comprehend, but when we really consider
who You are and what You've done for us,
how can we not both fear and love You?

Unquenchable Love

Many waters cannot quench love; rivers cannot sweep it away. If one were to give all the wealth of one's house for love, it would be utterly scorned.

SONG OF SOLOMON 8:7 NIV

Have you ever been so thirsty that a cup of water didn't satisfy you? If so, then you have some understanding of how love works. The more you have of it, the more you want. And God's love for us is so overpowering that nothing we do can wash it away. Talk about amazing love! Lift up your voice in praise for the love you've been shown.

Creation Speaks

*The heavens declare the glory
of God; and the firmament
shows His handiwork.*

PSALM 19:1 NKJV

We've traveled through several states recently and seen many scenic pictures. Golden fields, purple mountains, sparkling lakes. . . How could anyone believe that something so amazing just happened? Your awesome creation speaks the truth, and to You belongs all the glory!

Healthy Attitudes

*"No one can serve two masters;
for either he will hate the one and
love the other, or else he will be loyal
to the one and despise the other.
You cannot serve God and mammon."*

MATTHEW 6:24 NKJV

So often, Lord, I see relationships crumbling, and much of the time a money issue is what starts the process. Some people are careless or dishonest in their spending; others just want too much. As a result there is a lot of bitterness and hatred. Please help me to have a proper outlook when money is involved.

Sacrifice of Praise

*Be diligent in these matters; give
yourself wholly to them, so that
everyone may see your progress.*

1 TIMOTHY 4:15 NIV

Lord, may the life I live be a continual sacrifice of praise to You. You, who have done
so much for me, ask only that I give my life
wholly to You. How can I refuse? Let what
others see in me be cause for them to glorify
You, too.

He Will Guide Me

"So I say to you, ask, and it will be given to you; seek, and you will find; knock, and it will be opened to you. For everyone who asks receives, and he who seeks finds, and to him who knocks it will be opened."

LUKE 11:9–10 NKJV

I'm facing a situation right now, and I'm not quite sure how to handle it, Father. I'm coming to You because I truly lack wisdom, but I need to know how to make the right decision. Thank You for promising that You will guide me.

O Give Thanks

Oh, give thanks to the LORD, for He is good! For His mercy endures forever.

PSALM 136:1 NKJV

Father, I was working on a series of lessons for the children's Sunday school, and I felt led to concentrate on the verse that says, "O give thanks unto the LORD" (Psalm 136:1). I realized how many things we have to be thankful for and how many lessons in Your Word back this up. You are indeed worthy of our thanks!

White as Snow

Purge me with hyssop, and I shall be clean; wash me, and I shall be whiter than snow.

PSALM 51:7 NKJV

What a beautiful illustration of purity You've given us in a blanket of fresh-fallen snow. It's the kind of purity You want for my life, and it's the cleanliness that only You can give. I am so grateful for Your saving blood that washed my life white as snow.

At Peace with Others

*For the sake of my brethren
and companions, I will now say,
"Peace be within you."*

PSALM 122:8 NKJV

There are a lot of people with whom I must get along. We come from a variety of backgrounds, and we don't always agree on everything. I've found, however, that peaceful disagreement makes for better relationships, so help me to do my part to live peaceably with others.

Menial Tasks

*Commit your works to the LORD,
and your thoughts will be established.*

PROVERBS 16:3 NKJV

Do You ever wish we'd eliminate the
phrase "menial task" from our vocabulary,
Father? I know that all work is important
to You and that the attitude I have when
performing each duty holds even greater
weight. Help me to remember that even the
small jobs have significance in light of the
bigger picture.

God's in Control

*"For I know the plans I have for you,
declares the LORD, plans for welfare and
not for evil, to give you a future
and a hope."*

JEREMIAH 29:11 ESV

Thank You, Lord, that You have a perfect plan for my life. I know I don't always understand it, but You know what's best, and everything that happens is for a reason— that You might be glorified. I'm so glad that You are in control and that I need not worry.

Good Relationships

*Love each other with genuine affection,
and take delight in honoring each other.*
ROMANS 12:10 NLT

Thank You, Lord, for giving me a good
relationship with family. So many people
struggle with unhappy homes, and it's only
Your grace that protects me from that. I ask
that You'd keep Your hand on our home and
give others happy lives as well.

Evening Rainbows

And God said: "This is the sign of the covenant which I make between Me and you, and every living creature that is with you, for perpetual generations: I set My rainbow in the cloud, and it shall be for the sign of the covenant between Me and the earth."

GENESIS 9:12 NKJV

When I first caught a glimpse of that rainbow, I was thrilled. When I really stopped to look at its brilliance, I was awed. Only You could have painted something so glorious across the expanse of the evening sky. Thank You for the beauty of Your promises.

Entering God's Rest

"Come to Me, all you who labor and are heavy laden, and I will give you rest."

MATTHEW 11:28 NKJV

Dear Jesus, in this world, we will never experience true rest, but You've offered this tantalizing refreshment to anyone who will enter it. Yet so many reject this repose You offer. It's a refusal I can't fathom, Lord. Show them what they are missing. Draw them into Your rest today.

Affecting Others

*"Truly, truly, I say to you, whoever
believes in me will also do the works
that I do; and greater works than
these will he do, because I am
going to the Father."*

JOHN 14:12 ESV

Lately I've been feeling a little low, Father.
I'm not meeting those expectations I have
of myself, and I've been dragging myself
down. Unfortunately, my lack of self-
esteem is pulling others down, too. I don't
want to do that. I want to give my frustra-
tions to You and let You work through me.

A Servant's Heart

Therefore, my beloved brothers, be steadfast, immovable, always abounding in the work of the Lord, knowing that in the Lord your labor is not in vain.

1 CORINTHIANS 15:58 ESV

The irony in Your Word makes me smile, Lord. When You speak of greatness, it's in connection with servanthood. It's so contrary to human nature, but when I think about it, it really does make sense. That still doesn't make it easy though. Please give me a servant's heart.

The Beauty of Christ

Charm is deceptive, and beauty does not last; but a woman who fears the LORD will be greatly praised.

PROVERBS 31:30 NLT

You know, Lord, I spend a lot of time each morning trying to look physically attractive. That doesn't do much for my soul though. Sure, I feel better when I look nice; but I know if people saw Your beauty in me, that would bring more joy. Draw me close, and make this a reality.

Stress and Vulnerability

*Enter not into the path of the wicked,
and go not in the way of evil men.*

PROVERBS 4:14

Dear God, I've discovered that during
these times of stress I seem more vulnerable
to temptation. I need You even more
during this trying hour. I must lean on You
and on the godly friends You've provided.
Help me to focus on the goal, and keep me
from faltering.

Solomon's Choice

*But the wisdom that is from above
is first pure, then peaceable, gentle,
willing to yield, full of mercy and
good fruits, without partiality
and without hypocrisy.*

JAMES 3:17 NKJV

You gave Solomon an opportunity to ask
of You any gift he desired, and he asked
for wisdom. Thus he received many more
blessings. I'd like to think I would have
asked the same, but I don't know if I would
have. Please make me more spiritually mature so I'll ask for things that really matter.

God's Family

*Let us think of ways to motivate one
another to acts of love and good works.*

HEBREWS 10:24 NLT

As much as I love my family, I am infinitely
more grateful to be part of Your family. To
have other believers laugh and cry with me
is a beautiful picture of Your love. To be able
to pray with them, knowing You are in our
midst, is great joy. Thank You for making
me Your child.

Matchless Grace

And the Word was made flesh, and dwelt among us, (and we beheld His glory, the glory as of the only begotten of the Father,) full of grace and truth.

JOHN 1:14

The song talks of praising You for Your matchless grace, and how could I go through a single day without doing so? I don't understand why You love and forgive me, but I wish to offer my sincerest thanks for these bountiful gifts. You are a wonderful Savior!

Scripture Index

OLD TESTAMENT

Genesis
9:12. . . . . day 357

Deuteronomy
7:9. . . . . day 151
10:12. . . . . . . day 345
31:6. . . . . day 300

Joshua
1:9. . . . . day 270
22:5. . . . . day 204
24:15. . . . . . . day 296

2 Samuel
23:3–4 . . . . . day 343

1 Kings
8:61. . . . . day 1

1 Chronicles
16:9. . . . . day 143
29:11. . . . . . . day 308

2 Chronicles
20:17. . . . . . . day 334

Psalms
1:2. . . . . day 12
1:3. . . . . day 272
4:7. . . . . day 222
5:3. . . . . day 167
5:7. . . . . day 122
5:11. . . . . day 255
6:9. . . . . day 135
9:9–10. . . . . . . day 18
10:12. . . . . day 38
10:17. . . . . day 190
13:5–6 . . . . . day 112
16:2. . . . . . days 66, 92
16:3. . . . . day 31

16:5. . . . . day 86
16:6. . . . . . . day 186
16:7. . . . . . . day 174
16:11. . . . . . day 260
17:2. . . . . day 241
17:3. . . . . day 145
18:6. . . . . day 206
18:20. . . . . . . day 138
18:21. . . . . . . day 238
18:24. . . . . . . day 274
18:35. . . . . days 62, 78
19:1. . . . . day 347
19:4. . . . . day 147
19:11. . . . . . . day 160
19:13. . . . . day 91
19:14. . . . . . . day 131
20:4. . . . . day 141
20:7. . . . . day 144
22:28. . . . . . . day 315
23:1. . . . . day 22
23:2–3. . . . . . . day 208
23:6. . . . . days 72, 194
25:4. . . . . day 289
25:5. . . . . day 97

25:8. . . . . day 244
25:16. . . . . day 81
26:2. . . . . day 162
27:13. . . . . day 7
27:14. . . . . days 90, 99
28:7. . . . days 279, 331
29:2. . . . . day 133
29:11. . . . . . . day 335
30:5. . . . . day 121
30:11. . . . . day 46
31:6. . . . . day 211
31:14–15 . . . . day 276
31:24. . . . . day 27
32:1. . . . . day 197
32:7. . . . . day 158
32:8. . days 36, 68, 119
33:4. . . . . day 126
33:6. . . . . day 202
33:11. . . . days 16, 219
34:5. . . . . day 29
34:7. . . . . day 114
34:8. . . . . day 45
34:9. . . . . day 34
34:11. . . . . . . day 261

34:12. . . . . . . .day 193
34:18. . . . days 47, 216
35:9. . . . . .day 59
35:18. . . . . . . .day 182
35:27. . . . . . . .day 74
36:6. . . . . .day 128
37:4. . . . . days 94, 118
37:5. . . . . .day 104
37:7. . . . . .day 73
37:21. . . . . . . .day 248
37:24. . . . . . . .day 323
37:30. . . . days 43, 108
37:37. . . days 148, 191
38:9. . . . . .day 65
40:4. . . . . .day 153
42:2. . . . . .day 115
45:4. . . . . .day 198
46:1. . . . . .day 295
46:10. . . . . . . .day 132
49:16. . . . . . . .day 171
50:14. . . . . . . .day 224
51:6. . . . . .day 251
51:7. . . . . .day 352
51:10. . . . . . . .day 161

51:17. . . . . . . .day 123
52:8. . . . . .day 201
52:9. . . . . .day 56
55:16–17 . . . .day 281
55:22. . . . .days 53,140,
                340
56:8. . . . . .day 268
57:2. . . . . .day 217
57:7. . . . . .day 21
57:10. . . . . . . .day 249
59:9–10. . . . . .day 243
59:17. . . . . . . .day 109
61:5. . . . . .day 183
62:10. . . . . . . .day 58
62:12. . . . . . . .day 234
63:6. . . . . .day 130
63:7. . . . . .day 102
65:8. . . . . days 41, 152
67:1. . . . . .day 283
68:6. . . . . .day 54
68:19. . . . . . . .day 278
69:32. . . . . . . .day 64
71:7. . . . . .day 181
71:14. . . . . . . .day 165

73:26. . . . . day 49

76:11. . . . . day 269

77:20. . . . . day 42

78:4. . . . . day 215

84:5. . . . . day 275

84:10. . . . . day 84

84:11. . . . . . days 6, 35

85:10. . . . . . . day 111

86:2. . . . . day 169

86:4. . . . . day 127

86:5. . . . . day 30

86:15. . . . . day 240

89:1–2. . . . . . . day 311

90:2. . . . . day 11

90:12. . . . days 69, 149

90:14. . . . . day 124

90:17. . . . . day 185

91:1. . . . . day 263

92:1. . . . . day 142

94:18. . . . . day 195

94:19. . . . . day 100

95:1–2. . . . . day 229

98:1. . . . . day 223

99:3. . . . . day 258

100:1. . . . . day 230

100:2. . . . . day 264

101:2. . . . . day 254

100:5. . . . . day 55

103:2. . . . . day 67

103:5. . . . . day 116

103:6. . . . . day 257

103:11. . . . . day 71

103:12. . . . . . . day 101

103:13. . . . . day 20

105:3–4 . . . . . . day 37

105:8. . . . . day 87

106:3. . . . . day 210

107:8. . . . . day 293

107:42. . . . . . . day 271

111:10. . . . . . . day 336

112:5. . . . . day 61

112:6–8 . . . . . . day 88

112:7. . . . . day 154

115:14. . . . . . . day 209

116:6. . . . . day 51

116:7. . . . . day 13

118:8–9. . . . . . day 237

118:14. . . . . day 82

118:24. . . days 10, 306
119:1. . . . . . . .day 106
119:15. . . . . . . .day 96
119:32. . . . . days 172
119:45. . . . . . . .day 25
119:73. . . . . . .day 232
119:123. . . . . .day 196
119:129. . . . . .day 79
119:135. . . . . .day 312
119:175. . . . . .day 253
121:8. . . . . . . .day 14
122:8. . . . . . .day 353
125:1. . . . . . . .day 26
127:1. . . days 136, 227
127:3 . . . . days 17, 178,
179
128:2. . . . . . .day 267
128:3. . . . . . . .day 60
130:6. . . . . . .day 150
131:2. . . . . . .day 166
133:1. . . . . . .day 173
136:1. . . . . . .day 351
138:3. . . . days 23, 247
138:6. . . . . . .day 105
138:8. . . . . . .day 137

139:13. . . . . . .day 85
139:14. . . . . . . .day 9
139:16. . . . . . .day 32
139:18. . . . . .day 156
139:23. . . . . .day 265
141:3. . . . . . .day 157
143:10. . . . . . .day 50
144:12. . . . . .day 164
144:15. . . . . .day 107
145:2. . . . . . . .day 95
145:9. . . . . .day 2
145:13. . . . . .day 250
145:15. . . . . .day 170
145:16. . . . . .day 235
145:18. . . . days 83, 175,
203
146:3. . . . . . .day 192
146:5. . . . . . . .day 40
147:3. . . . . . .day 187
147:4. . . . . . .day 110
147:5–6 . . . . . .day 15
147:8. . . . . . .day 231
149:4. . . . . . .day 155

Proverbs

2:2. . . . . day 318
2:6. . . . . day 125
4:14. . . . . day 362
6:4. . . . . day 159
10:21. . . . . day 168
12:25. . . . . day 77
14:29. . . . . day 319
14:30. . . . . day 341
16:3. . . . . day 354
22:6. . . . . day 327
22:29. . . . . day 163
28:19–20. . . . . day 321
29:11. . . . . day 199
31:30. . . days 103, 361
31:31. . . . . day 292

Ecclesiastes

3:1. . . . . day 90
3:12–13. . . . . . day 288

Song of Solomon

4:7. . . . . day 117
8:7. . . . . day 346

Isaiah

26:3. . . . . day 344
43:4. . . . . . days 5, 225

Jeremiah

24:7. . . . . day 146
29:11. . . . . day 355

Lamentations

3:22–23. . days 93, 280

Daniel

10:19. . . . . day 316

Habakkuk

2:3. . . . . day 207

NEW TESTAMENT

Matthew

5:8. . . . . days 19, 301
5:14–16 . . . . . day 287
6:6. . . . . day 309

6:24. . . . . .day 348
6:27. . . . . .day 328
6:33. . . . . . days 4, 302
6:34. . . . . . . .day 330
7:12. . . . . . . .day 338
11:28. . . . . . . .day 358
11:29. . . . days 48, 277
22:37. . . days 228, 259

Mark
6:31. . . . . .day 159
10:15. . . . . . . .day 63
11:24. . . . . . . day 325
16:15. . . days 256, 339

Luke
5:16. . . . . .day 282
11:9–10. . . . . .day 350
12:15. . . . . . . .day 291
18:29–30. . . . .day 262
21:1–4 . . . . . .day 329

John
1:14. . . . . .day 365
3:16. . . . . .day 314

8:12. . . . . .day 286
13:5. . . . . .day 317
14:12. . . . . . .day 359
14:23. . . . . . .day 39
14:27. . . . . . .day 52
15:12. . . . . . .day 236
16:33 . . . . days 33, 249

Acts
1:14. . . . . .day 233
22:14. . . . . .day 8

Romans
8:28. . . . days 284, 294
8:37–39. . . . . .day 305
12:10. . . . . . . .day 356
12:12. . . . . . . .day 245
12:13. . . . . . . .day 221
12:16. . . . . . . .day 75

1 Corinthians
6:19–20. . . . . .day 120
13:4–7 . . . . . .day 333
13:7. . . . . .day 218
15:58 . . . . day 360

2 Corinthians

3:4–5 . . . . day 332
3:17 . . . . day 307
6:14 . . . . day 180
9:8 . . . . day 24
12:9 . . . . day 129

Ephesians

2:4-5 . . . . day 242
2:8 . . . . day 57
4:15 . . . . day 43
4:23 . . . . day 285
4:32 . . . . day 303
5:15 . . . . day 324
5:15–16 . . . . . day 322
5:30 . . . . day 3

Philippians

2:3 . . . . day 246
4:6 . . . . day 134
4:6-7 . . . . . . day 212
4:19 . . . . day 252

Colossians

3:12–14 . . . . . day 205
3:13 . . . . day 337
3:16 . . . . day 184
4:2 . . . . days 220, 226
4:5–6 . . . . day 342

1 Thessalonians

5:12–13 . . . . . day 189

1 Timothy

2:9–10 . . . . . . day 266
4:15 . . . . day 349
5:17 . . . . day 188
6:6 . . . . day 290

2 Timothy

2:15 . . . . day 310
2:21 . . . . day 89
2:23–24 . . . . . day 176
4:17–18 . . . . . day 297

Titus

3:5 . . . . day 28

Hebrews
10:24. . . . . day 364
10:24–25. . . . days 200,
                304
13:5. . . . . day 76

James
1:2–3. . . . . . . day 326
1:4. . . . . day 320
1:17. . . . . day 299
1:19–20 days 177, 214
3:17. . . . . day 363
4:8. . . . . page 5
5:13–15 . . . . . day 139

1 Peter
1:8. . . . . day 313
2:9. . . . . day 98
3:3–4 . . . . . . day 113
3:4. . . . . day 273
3:12. . . . . day 298
5:10. . . . . day 80

1 John
2:6. . . . . day 239
2:10. . . . . day 44
5:20. . . . . day 70

Revelation
3:8. . . . . day 213

Notes

_____

_____

_____

_____

_____

_____

_____

_____

_____

_____

_____

_____

_____

Notes

Notes

_____

_____

_____

_____

_____

_____

_____

_____

_____

_____

_____